# The
# Wiersbe

## BIBLE STUDY SERIES

EXODUS

# The
# Wiersbe
## BIBLE STUDY SERIES

Finding Freedom

by Following

God

David C Cook
*transforming lives together*

THE WIERSBE BIBLE STUDY SERIES: EXODUS
Published by David C Cook
4050 Lee Vance Drive
Colorado Springs, CO 80918 U.S.A.

Integrity Music Limited, a Division of David C Cook
Brighton, East Sussex BN1 2RE, England

The graphic circle C logo is a registered trademark of David C Cook.

All Scripture quotations in this study are taken from the Holy Bible, New
International Version®, NIV®. Copyright © 1973, 1984 by Biblica, Inc.™ Used by
permission of Zondervan. All rights reserved worldwide. www.zondervan.com.

In the *Be Delivered* excerpts, unless otherwise noted, all Scripture quotations are taken
from the King James Version of the Bible. (Public Domain.) Scripture quotations
marked NIV are taken from the *Holy Bible, New International Version®. NIV®*. Copyright
© 1973, 1978, 1984 by Biblica, Inc. Used by permission of Zondervan. All rights
reserved worldwide. www.zondervan.com; NKJV are taken from the New King James
Version. Copyright © 1982 by Thomas Nelson, Inc. Used by permission. All rights
reserved. The author has added italics in Scripture quotations for emphasis.

All excerpts taken from *Be Delivered*, second edition, published by David C
Cook in 2010 © 1998 Warren W. Wiersbe, ISBN 978-1-4347-6503-1.

ISBN 978-0-7814-0847-9
eISBN 978-1-4347-0598-3
LCCN 2013934252

The Team: Steve Parolini, Karen Lee-Thorp, Amy Konyndyk,
Nick Lee, Tonya Osterhouse, Karen Athen
Series Cover Design: John Hamilton Design

Printed in the United States of America
First Edition 2013

2 3 4 5 6 7 8 9 10

022819

# Contents

Introduction to Exodus. . . . . . . . . . . . . . . . . . . . . . . . . . . . . . . 7

How to Use This Study . . . . . . . . . . . . . . . . . . . . . . . . . . . . . . 9

**Lesson 1**
Deliverer (Exodus 1—4). . . . . . . . . . . . . . . . . . . . . . . . . . . . 13

**Lesson 2**
War (Exodus 5—10). . . . . . . . . . . . . . . . . . . . . . . . . . . . . . .31

**Lesson 3**
The Final Plague (Exodus 11:1—13:16) . . . . . . . . . . . . . . . . . 49

**Lesson 4**
Redeemed (Exodus 13:17—16:36) . . . . . . . . . . . . . . . . . . . . .65

**Lesson 5**
The Lord of Hosts (Exodus 17—18) . . . . . . . . . . . . . . . . . . . 83

**Lesson 6**
The Book (Exodus 19:1—24:8). . . . . . . . . . . . . . . . . . . . . . .101

**Lesson 7**
Where God Dwells (Exodus 24:9—27:21; 30—31; 35—38) . . . . .119

**Lesson 8**
Glory (Exodus 28—29; 32—34; 39—40) . . . . . . . . . . . . . . . .135

**Bonus Lesson**
Summary and Review . . . . . . . . . . . . . . . . . . . . . . . . . . . . . .155

# Introduction to Exodus

## Liberation

Whether it means freeing a nation from political bondage or delivering an individual from dependence or codependence, liberation is a popular theme these days.

But many people who want to be free don't really know what freedom is or how to use it if they have it. "Unless a man has the talents to make something of himself, freedom is an irksome burden," wrote the longshoreman and philosopher Eric Hoffer in *The True Believer*; and he is right. Fools use freedom as a toy to play with; wise people use freedom as a tool to build with.

## Privilege

Using the experiences of Israel as Exhibit A, the book of Exodus explains what true freedom is, what freedom costs, and how it must be used. Exodus teaches us that freedom is not license and discipline is not bondage. God tells us how to enjoy mature freedom in His will, a quality that is desperately needed in our churches and in our world today. The privilege of freedom is precious; the responsibilities of freedom are serious; and we can't have one without the other.

—*Warren W. Wiersbe*

# How to Use This Study

This study is designed for both individual and small-group use. We've divided it into eight lessons—each references one or more chapters in Warren W. Wiersbe's commentary *Be Delivered* (second edition, David C Cook, 2010). While reading *Be Delivered* is not a prerequisite for going through this study, the additional insights and background Wiersbe offers can greatly enhance your study experience.

The **Getting Started** questions at the beginning of each lesson offer you an opportunity to record your first thoughts and reactions to the study text. This is an important step in the study process as those "first impressions" often include clues about what it is your heart is longing to discover.

The bulk of the study is found in the **Going Deeper** questions. These dive into the Bible text and, along with helpful excerpts from Wiersbe's commentary, help you examine not only the original context and meaning of the verses but also modern application.

**Looking Inward** narrows the focus down to your personal story. These intimate questions can be a bit uncomfortable at times, but don't shy away from honesty here. This is where you are asked to stand before the mirror of God's Word and look closely at what you see. It's the place to take a good look at yourself in light of the lesson and search for ways in which you can grow in faith.

**Going Forward** is the place where you can commit to paper those things you want or need to do in order to better live out the discoveries you made in the Looking Inward section. Don't skip or skim through this. Take the time to really consider what practical steps you might take to move closer to Christ. Then share your thoughts with a trusted friend who can act as an encourager and accountability partner.

Finally, there is a brief **Seeking Help** section to close the lesson. This is a reminder for you to invite God into your spiritual-growth process. If you choose to write out a prayer in this section, come back to it as you work through the lesson and continue to seek the Holy Spirit's guidance as you discover God's will for your life.

## Tips for Small Groups

A small group is a dynamic thing. One week it might seem like a group of close-knit friends. The next it might seem more like a group of uncomfortable strangers. A small-group leader's role is to read these subtle changes and adjust the tone of the discussion accordingly.

Small groups need to be safe places for people to talk openly. It is through shared wrestling with difficult life issues that some of the greatest personal growth is discovered. But in order for the group to feel safe, participants need to know it's okay not to share sometimes. Always invite honest disclosure, but never force someone to speak if he or she isn't comfortable doing so. (A savvy leader will follow up later with a group member who isn't comfortable sharing in a group setting to see if a one-on-one discussion is more appropriate.)

Have volunteers take turns reading excerpts from Scripture or from the commentary. The more each person is involved even in the mundane tasks, the more they'll feel comfortable opening up in more meaningful ways.

The leader should watch the clock and keep the discussion moving. Sometimes there may be more Going Deeper questions than your group can cover in your available time. If you've had a fruitful discussion, it's okay to move on without finishing everything. And if you think the group is getting bogged down on a question or has taken off on a tangent, you can simply say, "Let's go on to question 5." Be sure to save at least ten to fifteen minutes for the Going Forward questions.

Finally, soak your group meetings in prayer—before you begin, during as needed, and always at the end of your time together.

# Deliverer
## (EXODUS 1—4)

*Before you begin …*
- *Pray for the Holy Spirit to reveal truth and wisdom as you go through this lesson.*
- *Read Exodus 1—4. This lesson references chapter 1 in* Be Delivered. *It will be helpful for you to have your Bible and a copy of the commentary available as you work through this lesson.*

## Getting Started

### From the Commentary

The Old Testament is God's "continued story" of His great program of salvation that He announced to Adam and Eve (Gen. 3:15) and to Abraham (12:1–3). That explains why the Hebrew text of Exodus begins with the word *and*, for God is continuing the story He started in Genesis. God's wonderful story finally led to the coming of Jesus to earth and His death on the cross, and it won't end until God's people go to heaven and see Jesus on the throne. What a story!

—*Be Delivered*, page 17

1. From its first four chapters, what does Exodus seem to be about? What role do you expect Moses to play in this story? How is this a continuation of the story God began with Adam and Eve? How does it lead to our story today?

*More to Consider: The Jewish rabbis call Exodus "the Book of Names" (or "These Are the Names"), because it opens with a list of the names of the sons of Jacob (Israel) who brought their families to Egypt to escape the famine in Canaan (Gen. 46). What is the significance of listing these names? What importance did names have in Moses' time? How did God use the Israelite's experiences in Egypt to prepare them for the tasks He gave them to accomplish on earth? What were those tasks?*

2. Choose one verse or phrase from Exodus 1—4 that stands out to you. This could be something you're intrigued by, something that makes you uncomfortable, something that puzzles you, something that resonates with you, or just something you want to examine further. Write that here.

## Going Deeper

*From the Commentary*

During the years Joseph served as second ruler in Egypt, his family was greatly respected, and even after Joseph died, his memory was honored in the way the Egyptians treated the Hebrews. God kept His covenant promise to Abraham by blessing his descendants and causing them to multiply greatly (Gen. 12:1–3; 15:5; 17:2, 6; 22:17). By the time of the exodus, there were more than 600,000 men who were twenty years and older (Ex. 12:37; 38:26), and when you add the women and children, the total could well be nearly two million people, all of whom descended

from the original family of Jacob. God certainly kept His
promise!

—*Be Delivered*, page 18

3. What was the new pharaoh's response to the rapid multiplication of the
Jewish people? What steps did he take to try to change their story? (See
Ex. 1:8–22.)

## From the Commentary

Amram and Jochebed were Moses' parents (Ex. 6:20),
and while the Exodus text emphasizes the faith of the
mother, Hebrews 11:23 commends both the father and
the mother for trusting God. Certainly it took faith for
them to have normal marital relations during that dangerous time when Jewish babies were being killed. Moses
became a great man of faith, and he learned it first from
his godly parents. Amram and Jochebed already had two
children: Miriam, who was the oldest, and Aaron, who
was three years older than Moses (Ex. 7:7).

From the very first, Moses was seen to be "no ordinary child" (Acts 7:20 NIV; see Heb. 11:23), and it was evident that God had a special purpose for him. Believing this to be true, the parents defied Pharaoh's edict and kept their son alive. This wasn't easy to do, since all the Egyptians were now Pharaoh's official spies, watching for babies to be drowned (Ex. 1:22).

—*Be Delivered*, pages 20–21

4. Review Exodus 2:1–10. How did Jochebed obey the letter of the law, but not necessarily the spirit of the law? What does this tell us about one of the many ways God works to accomplish His plan? What does this story teach us about the obstacles to faith? About God's role in helping us to overcome them?

### From the History Books

Exodus tells a story of a powerful leader attempting to control a people—the Jews. History (both ancient and modern) tells many similar stories—many of which are even more heinous. From Hitler's attempt to exterminate the very same people in World War II to the Rwandan genocide in 1994, the dehumanization of people has continued to plague our world in horrific and catastrophic ways. Even today there are governments intent on destroying or diminishing people solely based on religious or cultural disagreements.

5. How is the situation the Jews faced in captivity similar to the more recent attempts to eradicate a group of people? How is it different? What does this pharaoh's response to Moses teach us about the pharaoh's heart toward the Jewish people? Why didn't he simply try to destroy them, as so many nations had previously tried? What causes a leader or a nation to denigrate a people or culture? What should our response today be to such travesties?

## From the Commentary

> God used a baby's tears to control the heart of a powerful princess, and He used Miriam's words to arrange for the baby's mother to raise the boy and get paid for it! The phrase *as weak as a baby* doesn't apply in the kingdom of God, for when the Lord wants to accomplish a mighty work, He often starts by sending a baby. This was true when He sent Isaac, Joseph, Samuel, John the Baptist, and especially Jesus. God can use the weakest things to

defeat the mightiest enemies (1 Cor. 1:25–29). A baby's tears were God's first weapons in His war against Egypt.

The princess adopted Moses as her own son, which means that Moses had a favored position in the land and was given a special education for service in the government (Acts 7:22). In the Egyptian language, Moses means "born" or "son" and sounds like a Hebrew word that means "to draw out" (of the water). Years later, his name would remind Moses of the God who rescued him and did great things for him in Egypt. On more than one occasion, Moses would rescue his people because he trusted the Lord.

—*Be Delivered*, page 21

6. Why does God so often speak to His nation through a baby or a child? What does this teach us about God's character? What does it tell us about His love for His greatest creation? What does it tell us about how we ought to treat one another—young or old?

## From the Commentary

Moses spent his first forty years (Acts 7:23) serving in the Egyptian bureaucracy. (Some students think he was being groomed to be the next pharaoh.) Egypt seems the least likely place for God to start training a leader, but God's ways are not our ways. In equipping Moses for service, God took several approaches. The first of these was education.

"And Moses was learned in all the wisdom of the Egyptians, and was mighty in words and deeds" (Acts 7:22 NKJV). What did that involve? Egypt had a highly developed civilization for its time, particularly in the areas of engineering, mathematics, and astronomy. Thanks to their knowledge of astronomy, they developed an amazingly accurate calendar, and their engineers planned and supervised the construction of edifices that are still standing. Their priests and doctors were masters of the art of embalming, and their leaders were skilled in organization and administration. Visitors to Egypt today can't help but be impressed with the accomplishments of this ancient people. The servant of God should learn all he can, dedicate it to God, and faithfully serve God.

—*Be Delivered*, page 22

7. Review Exodus 2:11–14. Why was it important that Moses knew the Egyptians' ways? How was this crucial to his relationship with the pharaoh? To his calling to serve God? Why was education important to

the Egyptians? To Moses? What does this teach us about the importance of educating ourselves today?

## From the Commentary

Moses became a fugitive and fled to the land of the Midianites, relatives of the Jews (Gen. 25:1–2). True to his courageous nature, he assisted the daughters of Reuel, the priest of Midian (Ex. 2:18), and this led to hospitality in their home and marriage with one of the daughters, Zipporah, who bore him a son. Later, she would bear another son, Eliezer (18:1–4; 1 Chron. 23:15). Reuel ("friend of God") was also known as Jethro (Ex. 3:1; 18:12, 27), but Jethro ("excellence") may have been his title as priest rather than his given name.

The man who was "mighty in word and deed" is now in the lonely pastures taking care of stubborn sheep, but that was just the kind of preparation he needed for leading a nation of stubborn people. Israel was God's special flock (Ps. 100:3) and Moses His chosen shepherd. Like Joseph's thirteen years as a slave in Egypt and Paul's three years' hiatus after his conversion (Gal. 1:16–17), Moses' forty

years of waiting and working prepared him for a lifetime
of faithful ministry.

—*Be Delivered*, page 23

8. Review Exodus 2:15–25. Why did Moses because a fugitive? How was
this preparation for his later role? What does this reveal about how God
often works with the people He calls to lead? Why does it often take so
much time for God to train His leaders?

## From the Commentary

Moses spent forty years serving as a shepherd in Midian
(Acts 7:23; Ex. 7:7), and during those many days and
nights in the field, he no doubt meditated on the things
of God and prayed for his people who were suffering
in Egypt. It's significant that God calls people who are
busy: Gideon was threshing grain (Judg. 6), Samuel was
serving in the tabernacle (1 Sam. 3), David was caring
for sheep (17:20), Elisha was plowing (1 Kings 19:19–21),
four of the apostles were managing their fishing business
(Mark 1:16–20), and Matthew was collecting taxes (Matt.

9:9). God has nothing good to say about laziness (Prov. 24:30–34; Matt. 25:26–27; 2 Thess. 3:10–12).

**What Moses saw (vv. 1–4).** God can take an insignificant bush, ignite it, and turn it into a miracle, and that's what He wanted to do with Moses. Some see in the burning bush a picture of the nation of Israel: They are God's light in the world, persecuted but not consumed. But the burning bush was also a picture of what God had planned for Moses: He was the weak bush, but God was the empowering fire (Ex. 19:18; 24:17; Deut. 4:24; Judg. 13:20; Heb. 12:29), and with God's help, Moses could accomplish anything.

**What Moses heard (vv. 5–10).** God spoke to Moses and assured him that He was the God of his fathers and that He felt the suffering of the Jews in Egypt. He was now ready to deliver them out of Egypt and lead them into the Promised Land, and Moses would be His chosen leader. God's statement "Behold, I will send you" must have astonished Moses. Why would God choose a failure?

**What Moses did (3:1—4:17).** Moses should have rejoiced because God was at last answering prayer, and he should have submitted to God's will saying, "Here I am! Send me!" But instead, he argued with the Lord and tried to escape the divine call to rescue Israel from slavery.

—*Be Delivered*, pages 24–25

9. What reasons did Moses give for not being able to accept God's call? (See 3:11—4:17.) How is this similar to the way some believers respond to God today? Why are we so hesitant to do God's work? What role does faith play in all of this?

*More to Consider: God knows us better than we know ourselves, so we must trust Him and obey what He tells us to do. Read Judges 6:15, 1 Samuel 9:21, and Jereremiah 1:6. How are these stories similar to Moses' story? Why are we quick to tell God our weaknesses when He already knows them? How does the following statement answer Moses' (and our) excuse: The will of God will never lead you where the power of God can't enable you.*

## From the Commentary

When you've lived in a place for forty years, how do you go about packing up and moving elsewhere, especially when you're going to a place of danger? The text describes five encouragements God gave Moses as he sought to obey the will of God.

**(1) His father-in-law's blessing (4:18).** Moses couldn't leave without first informing his father-in-law and receiving his permission and blessing.

**(2) The promises of God (vv. 19–23).** As Moses stepped out by faith, God spoke to him and encouraged him. God told Moses not to be afraid to return to Egypt, because his enemies were dead. Then He assured Moses that He would enable him to do the miraculous signs but that Pharaoh would only harden his heart and thereby invite more judgments from the Lord.

**(3) Zipporah's obedience (vv. 24–26).** The servant of the Lord must be careful to "manage his own family well" (1 Tim. 3:4 NIV) if he expects to enjoy the blessings of the Lord; for "[i]f anyone does not know how to manage his own family, how can he take care of God's church?" (v. 5 NIV).

**(4) Aaron's arrival (vv. 27–28).** When it comes to serving the Lord, two are better than one (Eccl. 4:9). In spite of his faults, and we all have a few, Aaron ministered along with Moses and became the founder of the priesthood in Israel.

**(5) The nation's faith (vv. 29–31).** Moses had expressed fear that the Jewish elders wouldn't believe his message or accept his leadership, but they did, and so did the rest of the nation when they saw the demonstration of God's power in the signs. On hearing that God was concerned for them and was about to rescue them, they bowed in grateful worship.

—*Be Delivered*, pages 27–29

10. Why was it so important for God to give these encouragements to Moses? What kinds of encouragements does a church need to move forward into "places of danger"? What are those dangerous places? Why might God want the church to go there?

## Looking Inward

Take a moment to reflect on all that you've explored thus far in this study of Exodus 1—4. Review your notes and answers, and think about how each of these things matters in your life today.

*Tips for Small Groups: To get the most out of this section, form pairs or trios and have group members take turns answering these questions. Be honest and as open as you can in this discussion, but most of all, be encouraging and supportive of others. Be sensitive to those who are going through particularly difficult times and don't press for people to speak if they're uncomfortable doing so.*

11. Moses' very life was saved because someone defied a pharaoh (though she abided by the letter of the law in the process). Have you ever felt led to defy a law or an authority in order to accomplish God's purpose? Explain. Upon reflection, was your interpretation of God's intent correct? Were

there other ways to accomplish the same thing? What is the line that God draws when it comes to disobeying authorities?

12. What are some areas of your life today where you see God's delay? How might God be using this delay? What can you learn from it?

13. What has God called you to do that you are hesitant to act upon? Why are you hesitating? How does God's call on your life reveal your level of faith? How does accepting that call grow your faith? Grow you closer to God?

## Going Forward

14. Think of one or two things that you have learned that you'd like to work on in the coming week. Remember that this is all about quality, not quantity. It's better to work on one specific area of life and do it well than to work on many and do poorly (or to be so overwhelmed that you simply don't try).

Do you want to lean to trust God's specific call upon your life? Be specific. Go back through Exodus 1—4 and put a star next to the phrase or verse that is most encouraging to you. Consider memorizing this verse.

*Real-Life Application Ideas: Spend time this week considering God's call upon your life. Do you know what He's calling you to do? Have you responded to that call? If you don't know what God is calling you to do, talk with family members, trusted friends, and leaders in your church community. The perspectives offered by others can often clarify blurry issues relating to God's call. God may have used a burning bush in Moses' story—but he might use the people around you in yours. If you haven't yet embraced the call you discover in your life, start making specific plans to do so.*

## Seeking Help

15. Write a prayer below (or simply pray one in silence) inviting God to work on your mind and heart in those areas you've noted in the Going Forward section. Be honest about your desires and fears.

*Notes for Small Groups:*

- *Look for ways to put into practice the things you wrote in the Going Forward section. Talk with other group members about your ideas and commit to being accountable to one another.*

- *During the coming week, ask the Holy Spirit to continue to reveal truth to you from what you've read and studied.*

- *Before you start the next lesson, read Exodus 5—10. For more in-depth lesson preparation, read chapters 2, "War Is Declared," and 3, "'The Lord, Mighty in Battle,'" in* Be Delivered.

# War

## (EXODUS 5—10)

*Before you begin ...*

- *Pray for the Holy Spirit to reveal truth and wisdom as you go through this lesson.*
- *Read Exodus 5—10. This lesson references chapters 2 and 3 in* Be Delivered. *It will be helpful for you to have your Bible and a copy of the commentary available as you work through this lesson.*

## Getting Started

### From the Commentary

If Moses and Aaron had been privileged to listen to Jonathan Edwards preach his famous sermon "Sinners in the Hands of an Angry God," they probably would have shouted "Amen!" when Edwards said:

All the kings of the earth, before God, are as grasshoppers; they are nothing, and less than nothing: both their love and their hatred is to be despised. The wrath of the great King of kings, is as much more terrible than theirs, as his majesty is greater.

Hearing those words, Moses and Aaron would have recalled the day they stood before the ruler of one of the greatest kingdoms of the ancient world. They were sent by God to inform Pharaoh that if he didn't release the Jewish people, Jehovah would declare war on him and his gods and wouldn't stop attacking Egypt until the people of Israel were set free. God's two ambassadors had one message from the Lord: "Let My people go—or else!" Pharaoh's responses to Moses and Aaron were predictable: He rejected God's command, disdained the miracles Moses and Aaron performed, and deliberately hardened his heart against the Lord.

—*Be Delivered*, page 33

1. Why did God choose to threaten war against the Egyptian people instead of using a nonviolent approach to solve the Jewish captivity? What message did this deliver to the Egyptians? And yet they still rejected the request. What did this say about Pharaoh and his beliefs about the Jewish God?

2. Choose one verse or phrase from Exodus 5—10 that stands out to you. This could be something you're intrigued by, something that makes you uncomfortable, something that puzzles you, something that resonates with you, or just something you want to examine further. Write that here.

## Going Deeper

*From the Commentary*

> Their request was a simple one: Moses and Aaron wanted permission to take the Jewish people on a three-days' journey into the desert to a place where they could worship the Lord. Six days of travel and one day of worship would add up to a week away from their work, but Moses said nothing about how long they would be gone or when they would return. This omission made Pharaoh suspicious, and he wondered if the purpose of their journey was escape rather than worship. Three questions are involved in this episode.

**(1) Pharaoh: "Why should I obey the Lord?" (5:1–3).**

**(2) Pharaoh: "Why should the work stop?" (vv. 4–21).**

**(3) Moses: "Why have You sent me?" (5:22—6:27).**

*—Be Delivered*, pages 34–35

3. Review the three questions noted above. How was each of these questions critical to the Jewish people's ongoing saga? What did Pharaoh's questions reveal about his understanding of the Jewish God? What did Moses' question reveal about his own understanding and relationship with God? How are these questions relevant today?

*More to Consider: The genealogy (6:14–27) isn't there by accident, for it's the Lord's way of reminding us, the readers, that He had prepared Moses and Aaron for their ministry in Egypt. Their arrival in Jacob's family was part of His providential working. Reuben was Jacob's firstborn, then Simeon, and then Levi, the ancestor of Moses and Aaron. Read Jereremiah 1:5; Ephesians 2:10; Philippians 1:6. How do these verses speak to the idea of God's calling? To the manner in which God prepares people for His plan? How do they apply to Moses' story?*

## From the Commentary

> Up to this point in their confrontation with Pharaoh, Moses and Aaron had simply delivered God's ultimatum. Now the time had come for them to reveal God's power and perform the miraculous signs that proved they were truly sent by God. Still somewhat discouraged, Moses maintained that he wasn't a competent speaker, so God reminded him that Aaron could be his spokesman (Ex. 6:26—7:2; 4:15–16). However, the Lord advised Moses and Aaron that it would take more than one or two miracles to accomplish His purposes, for He would multiply His signs and wonders in the land of Egypt.
>
> Before we study this remarkable series of miracles, we must focus on the reasons why the Lord took this approach in dealing with Pharaoh and sent these sign judgments to the land of Egypt. The ultimate purpose, of course, was to bring Pharaoh and the Egyptians to their knees so they'd be willing for the Jews to leave the land. But at the same time, the Lord was revealing Himself to both the Israelites and the Egyptians and proving that He alone is God (7:5).
>
> —*Be Delivered*, page 38

4. Review Exodus 6:28—8:7. What lessons did God hope for the Egyptians to learn through these miracles? In what ways were the miracles a way of judging the gods of Egypt? Why was Pharaoh still so reluctant to see the truth of the one true God?

## From the Commentary

The three sign miracles that we're considering—the staff turned into a serpent, the water turned to blood, and the invasion of the frogs—have in common the fact that all of them were duplicated by Pharaoh's court magicians. Perhaps "counterfeited" is a more accurate word, because what they did was more likely deceptive sleight of hand. However, Satan can empower his people to perform "lying wonders" (2 Thess. 2:9–10; Matt. 24:24; Rev. 13:11–15), and that may have been the source of their power.

The apostle Paul used these Egyptian magicians to teach an important truth: In the last days, Satan will attack God's truth and God's people *by imitating the works of God*. Paul even named two of the court magicians: "Just as Jannes and Jambres opposed Moses, so also these men oppose the truth" (2 Tim. 3:8 NIV). As Jesus taught in the parable of the tares (Matt. 13:24–30, 36–43), Satan is a counterfeiter who "plants" imitation Christians in this world. Paul called them "false brethren" (2 Cor. 11:26). Satan has an imitation gospel (Gal. 1:6–9), a counterfeit righteousness (Rom. 10:1–3), and even counterfeit ministers who spread his lies (2 Cor. 11:13–15). Satan will one day produce a false Christ who will deceive the whole world (2 Thess. 2:1–12).

—*Be Delivered*, page 39

5. What made it especially challenging for Moses and Aaron to convince Pharaoh through these plagues that God was the only true God? How does Satan's imitation of God's work minimize the power and glory of God's work today? Do we see this happen in today's church? Explain.

## From the Commentary

Pharaoh began to harden his heart when Moses and Aaron performed the first miraculous sign before him, just as God said he would do (Ex. 7:3, 13–14). He hardened his heart further when his magicians counterfeited the signs

(v. 22) and even when they couldn't duplicate what Moses and Aaron had done (8:19). When Moses succeeded in stopping the plague of frogs, Pharaoh's heart again hardened (v. 15). This hardening continued throughout the entire series of plagues (v. 32; 9:7, 34–35; 13:15).

—*Be Delivered*, page 41

6. What does it mean to harden your heart? Why did Pharaoh harden his heart? What role did God Himself play in the hardening of Pharaoh's heart? (See 4:21; 7:3; 9:12; 10:1, 20, 27; 11:10; 14:4, 8, 17.) Why would God harden someone's heart? How is this significant in the ongoing narrative of God's plan for His people?

*From the Commentary*

God is gracious and longsuffering, but there comes a time when He will no longer tolerate the disobedience and arrogance of defiant sinners. "To the faithful you show yourself faithful, to the blameless you show yourself blameless, to the pure you show yourself pure, but to the crooked you show yourself shrewd" (Ps. 18:25–26 NIV).

If we walk contrary to Him, He will walk contrary to us (Lev. 26:23–24).

"God shows Himself to each individual according to his character," wrote Charles Spurgeon, and no individual in Scripture illustrates this truth better than the king of Egypt. For months, Moses and Aaron had dealt with Pharaoh, but the king was unwilling to obey God's command or even acknowledge God's authority. The water courses in Egypt had been turned into blood, slimy frogs had invaded the land, and swarms of pesky gnats had irritated the people, but Pharaoh had refused to bend.

What did God do? He declared all-out war on both the ruler of Egypt and the gods of Egypt. The Lord sent six painful and destructive plagues to the land, and then a seventh plague, which brought the death of every first-born son.

—*Be Delivered*, page 47

7. What can you conclude about Pharaoh's spiritual and moral states from his responses to the plagues? What price did he pay for his rebellion? What message is there in this story for those today who are unwilling to submit to God?

*From the Commentary*

> At certain times of the year, Pharaoh would go to the
> sacred Nile River to participate in special religious rites,
> and it certainly must have irritated him on that particular
> holy occasion to see Moses and Aaron waiting for him. In
> Pharaoh's eyes, these two men were national nuisances.
> Actually, Pharaoh was the cause of the nation's troubles,
> but he would not admit it. God was dealing with Pharaoh
> in mercy, wanting to bring him into submission, for it's
> only when we obey God that we can truly enjoy His bless-
> ings. With one blow, God could have wiped out Pharaoh
> and the nation (Ex. 9:15), but He chose to give them
> opportunity to repent.
>
> —*Be Delivered*, page 48

8. Review Exodus 8:20–32. How did God deal with Pharaoh in mercy?
How were the plagues a form of mercy to Pharaoh and his nation? Why
did God want to preserve the nation of Egypt at all?

*More to Consider: What are some of the "Egyptian compromises" we face today as we seek to serve the Lord? Read God's reply in 2 Corinthians 6:14–18; James 1:27 and 4:4. What do these passages tell us about what true service to God means? What are the dangers of negotiating the will of God to see how close we can get to the world?*

### From the Commentary

As you study the account of the plagues of Egypt, keep in mind the purposes God was fulfilling through these momentous events. First of all, He was manifesting His power to Pharaoh and his officials and proving to them that He alone is the true and living God. At the same time, the Lord was exposing the futility of the Egyptian religion and the vanity of the many gods they worshipped, including Pharaoh himself. All that God did to Egypt was a reminder to His people that their God was fighting for them and they didn't have to worry or be afraid.

—*Be Delivered*, page 51

9. How did each of the fifth through ninth plagues speak of God's power? His grace? His long-suffering? Why didn't Pharaoh bend to any of these plagues?

## From the Commentary

We don't know how long after the locusts left Egypt that God sent the ninth plague, but the darkness over the land for three days proved that Jehovah was greater than Ra (or Re) and Horus, both of whom the Egyptians revered as sun gods. The darkness wasn't the natural result of a sandstorm but was a miracle from the hand of the God of the Hebrews. There was light for the Israelites in the land of Goshen, just as there would be light for them as they marched out of Egypt (Ex. 14:19–20). The people of the world (Egypt) walk in the darkness, but the people of God walk in the light (John 3:19–21; 1 John 1:5–10).

Always ready to call for help when he was in trouble, Pharaoh summoned Moses and Aaron and made one more offer. The Jews could go on their journey to worship the Lord, but they couldn't take their flocks and herds with them. Pharaoh's plan was to confiscate all their livestock to replace what he had lost in the plagues, and then send his army to bring the Jews back to Egyptian slavery. Moses and Aaron rejected the offer, not only because they saw through his crafty plan, but because they knew that Israel had to obey all the will of God.

Pharaoh was a proud man, and proud people don't like to be outwitted by those whom they consider their inferiors. Moses and Aaron had refused his four offers and had insisted that he let the Israelites go. These two humble Jews had proved themselves more powerful than the exalted Pharaoh of Egypt, a son of the gods. By His mighty judgments, the God of the Hebrews had brought the great nation of Egypt to its knees, and both the leaders and the common people in the land held Moses in high regard (Ex. 11:3).

—*Be Delivered*, page 57

10. In what ways was Pharaoh a beaten man? Why wouldn't he admit it? What does this teach us about the dangerous nature of pride?

## Looking Inward

Take a moment to reflect on all that you've explored thus far in this study of Exodus 5—10. Review your notes and answers and think about how each of these things matters in your life today.

*Tips for Small Groups: To get the most out of this section, form pairs or trios and have group members take turns answering these questions. Be honest and as open as you can in this discussion, but most of all, be encouraging and supportive of others. Be sensitive to those who are going through particularly difficult times and don't press for people to speak if they're uncomfortable doing so.*

11. Have you ever experienced a hardened heart? What caused that? How did your heart finally soften? What did you learn during that season?

12. What are some ways you're tempted to negotiate the will of God so you can have more of the world? Why is it so hard to simply trust God, even when it means giving up things of this world that you desire? Where can you turn to find the strength to trust God and avoid negotiating His will?

13. What are some ways you struggle with pride? What causes that pride? Why is pride a problem? How can friends, family members, and the church help you to defeat pride?

## Going Forward

14. Think of one or two things that you have learned that you'd like to work on in the coming week. Remember that this is all about quality, not quantity. It's better to work on one specific area of life and do it well than to work on many and do poorly (or to be so overwhelmed that you simply don't try).

Do you want to go to battle with your pride? Be specific. Go back through Exodus 5—10 and put a star next to the phrase or verse that is most encouraging to you. Consider memorizing this verse.

*Real-Life Application Ideas: Pharaoh had a hard time admitting defeat, even though he and his people were suffering from God's punishments. Think about an area of your own life where you're stubbornly holding onto something that God wants you to let go. It could be something at work, a relational challenge, or even something specific to your spiritual walk. If you can't think of anything on your own, ask a spouse or trusted friend. We are often blind to our own stubbornness. Spend time in prayer, asking God to soften your heart and give you the strength to let go of that thing so you can move forward in your faith.*

## Seeking Help

15. Write a prayer below (or simply pray one in silence) inviting God to work on your mind and heart in those areas you've noted in the Going Forward section. Be honest about your desires and fears.

*Notes for Small Groups:*

- *Look for ways to put into practice the things you wrote in the Going Forward section. Talk with other group members about your ideas and commit to being accountable to one another.*

- *During the coming week, ask the Holy Spirit to continue to reveal truth to you from what you've read and studied.*

- *Before you start the next lesson, read Exodus 11:1— 13:16. For more in-depth lesson preparation, read chapter 4, "One More Plague," in* Be Delivered.

# The Final Plague
## (EXODUS 11:1—13:16)

*Before you begin …*
- *Pray for the Holy Spirit to reveal truth and wisdom as you go through this lesson.*
- *Read Exodus 11:1—13:16. This lesson references chapter 4 in* Be Delivered. *It will be helpful for you to have your Bible and a copy of the commentary available as you work through this lesson.*

## Getting Started

*From the Commentary*

This section of the book of Exodus focuses on an unpopular subject: death. King Jehovah (Ps. 95:3) was about to confront King Pharaoh with another king—death, the "king of terrors" (Job 18:14). The last enemy, death (1 Cor. 15:26), would visit Egypt with one last plague and deliver one last blow to the proud ruler of the land. In one solemn night, all the firstborn sons and all the firstborn livestock in Egypt would die, and there would be a great cry throughout the land (Ex. 11:6; 12:30). Only then would Pharaoh let God's people go.

However, death wouldn't visit the Jews and their livestock in the land of Goshen, because the Israelites belonged to the Lord and were His special people. In the land of Goshen, all that would die would be innocent yearling lambs, one for each Jewish household. This night would mark the inauguration of Passover, Israel's first national feast.

—*Be Delivered*, page 61

1. Why did this story have to be about death at all? What message was God delivering to both the Egyptians and the Jews through the role death played?

2. Choose one verse or phrase from Exodus 11:1—13:16 that stands out to you. This could be something you're intrigued by, something that makes you uncomfortable, something that puzzles you, something that resonates with you, or just something you want to examine further. Write that here.

# Going Deeper

## *From the Commentary*

> The people of Egypt had been irritated by the first six plagues, and their land and possessions had been devastated by the next two plagues. The ninth plague, the three days of darkness, had set the stage for the most dreadful plague of all, when the messengers of death would visit the land. "He unleashed against them his hot anger, his wrath, indignation and hostility—a band of destroying angels" (Ps. 78:49 NIV).
>
> *—Be Delivered*, pages 61–62

3. What is significant about the events between Pharaoh's last offer to Moses (10:24–29) and Moses' departure from the palace (10:29; 11:8)? What might have been going through Moses' mind when God told him He would send one more plague? What might Moses have been feeling up until that tenth plague was announced?

*More to Consider: Moses told the Jewish people that the time had come for them to collect their unpaid wages for all the work they and their ancestors had done as slaves in Egypt. Read Genesis 15:14 and Exodus 3:21–22. What do these verses tell us about God's promise to the Jews? How did this promise apply to the Jews' earnings in Egypt? Did the Jews intend to return what the Egyptians gave them? Explain.*

## From the Commentary

Moses warned Pharaoh in 11:4–10. This was Moses' final address to Pharaoh, who rejected it just as he did the other warnings. Pharaoh had no fear of God in his heart; therefore, he didn't take Moses' words seriously. But in rejecting God's word, Pharaoh caused the finest young men in the land to die and therefore brought profound sorrow to himself and to his people.

Two questions must be addressed at this point: (1) Why did God slay only the firstborn? (2) Was He just in doing so when Pharaoh was the true culprit? In answering the first question, we also help to answer the second.

In most cultures, firstborn sons are considered special, and in Egypt, they were considered sacred. We must remember that God calls Israel His firstborn son (Ex. 4:22; Jer. 31:9; Hos. 11:1). At the very beginning of their conflict, Moses warned Pharaoh that the way he treated God's firstborn would determine how God treated Egypt's firstborn (Ex. 4:22– 23).

*—Be Delivered, pages 62–63*

4. How was God's decision to slay the firstborn an example of paying Pharaoh back with his own currency? Why hadn't the plagues swayed Pharaoh? If God knew that they wouldn't change Pharaoh's hardened heart, why did He send each of them anyway?

## From Today's World

Pharaoh seemed to be playing a bit of a game with Moses during the plagues. For each plague God sent, Pharaoh had an answer. And he was quick to deny any power that Moses claimed came from his God. In the business world, this sort of game playing is equally common. When two strong-minded leaders butt heads, it's almost like they're playing a game of chicken to see who will break first. There's something in our humanness that makes us want to be right, even when the evidence suggests we're in the wrong. This has led to plenty of business failures, but also to failures in churches and especially in relationships. Today's "I'm right, and I'm going to stick to that belief at any cost" mentality is causing great harm.

5. Why do we have a hard time accepting when we're wrong? Where is pride a problem in our culture today? How does humility defeat pride? What does it take for a leader, a church, a spouse to embrace humility?

## From the Commentary

As to the justice of this tenth plague, who can pass judgment on the acts of the Lord when "righteousness and justice are the foundation of [His] throne" (Ps. 89:14 NIV)? But why should one man's resistance to God cause the death of many innocent young men? However, similar events happen in our world today. How many men and women who died in uniform had the opportunity to vote for or against a declaration of war? And as to the "innocence" of these firstborn sons, only God knows the human heart and can dispense His justice perfectly. "Shall not the Judge of all the earth do right?" (Gen. 18:25).

Pharaoh and the Egyptian people sinned against a flood of light and insulted God's mercy. The Lord had endured with much longsuffering the rebellion and arrogance of the king of Egypt as well as his cruel treatment of the Jewish people. God had warned Pharaoh many times, but the man wouldn't submit. Jehovah had publicly humiliated the Egyptian gods and goddesses and proved Himself to be the only true and living God, yet the nation would not believe.

—*Be Delivered*, pages 63–64

6. How did the tenth plague prove what the previous nine didn't? Why didn't God simply deliver that tenth plague first, and solve the crisis immediately? What lessons are there in God's long-suffering that we can apply to our circumstances today?

*From the Commentary*

> Passover marked a new beginning for the Jews and bound them together as a nation. When the Lord liberates you from bondage, it's the dawning of a new day and the beginning of a new life. Whenever you meet the words *redeem* or *redemption* in the New Testament, they speak of freedom from slavery. (There were an estimated sixty million slaves in the Roman Empire.) Jewish believers would immediately think of Passover and Israel's deliverance from Egypt through the blood of the lamb.
>
> The Jewish nation in the Old Testament had two calendars, a civil calendar that began in our September–October, and a religious calendar that began in our March–April. New Year's Day in the civil year ("Rosh Hashana"—"beginning of the year") fell in the seventh month of the religious calendar and ushered in the special events in the month of Tishri: the Feast of Trumpets, the Day of Atonement, and the Feast of Tabernacles. But Passover marked the beginning of the religious year, and at Passover, the focus is on the lamb.
>
> —*Be Delivered*, pages 64–65

7. In what way did Isaac's question (Gen. 22:7) introduce one of the major themes of the Old Testament? How was that question reiterated in the message delivered by the tenth plague?

## From the Commentary

On the fourteenth day of the month, at evening, *the lamb was slain* (Ex. 12:6b–7, 12–13, 21–24) and its blood was applied to the lintel and side posts of the doors of the houses in which the Jewish families lived. It wasn't the *life* of the lamb that saved the people from judgment, but the *death* of the lamb. Some people who claim to admire the life and teachings of Jesus don't want the cross of Jesus, yet it's His death on the cross that paid the price of our redemption (Matt. 20:28; 26:28; John 3:14–17; 10:11; Eph. 1:7; 1 Tim. 2:5–6; Heb. 9:28; Rev. 5:9). Jesus was our substitute; He died our death for us and suffered the judgment of our sin (Isa. 53:4–6; 1 Peter 2:24).

However, to be effective, the blood had to be applied to the doorposts; for God promised, "[W]hen I see the blood, I will pass over you" (Ex. 12:13). It isn't sufficient simply to know that Christ was sacrificed for the sins of the world (John 3:16; 1 John 2:2). We must appropriate that sacrifice for ourselves and be able to say with Paul, "The Son of God, who loved me, and gave himself for me" (Gal. 2:20), and with Mary, "My spirit has rejoiced in God my Savior" (Luke 1:46–47 NKJV). Our appropriation of the Atonement must be personal: "My LORD and my God" (John 20:28).

—*Be Delivered*, page 66

8. What is the significance of the symbolism of the lamb? (See Heb. 9:22; Lev. 17:11.) Why did the blood have to be applied to the doorposts? Wouldn't God have known whom to pass over? What was the lesson in that act?

*More to Consider: The Jews dipped flimsy hyssop plants into the basins of blood and applied the blood to the doorposts (Ex. 12:22). Read 24:1–8; and Leviticus 14:4, 6, 49, 51–52. How is hyssop used in these verses? How is our faith like hyssop?*

## From the Commentary

We usually call this event "the Jewish Passover," but the Bible calls it "the LORD's Passover" (Ex. 12:11, 27; Lev. 23:5; Num. 28:16). The observance was more than an "Independence Day" celebration, because the feast was kept "unto the LORD" (Ex. 12:48; Num. 9:10, 14). "It is the sacrifice of the LORD's passover" (Ex. 12:27). The focus of attention is on the Lord because what occurred that special night was because of Him. At least seventeen times in Exodus 12 "the LORD" is mentioned because He was the one in charge.

—*Be Delivered*, page 69

9. Underline all the mentions of "the Lord" in Exodus 12. What are some ways God established He was in charge? How did God reveal His power? How did He keep His promises? How did He deliver His people? (See 12:29–42, 51.)

## From the Commentary

We must never forget that it was the once timid and excuse-making Moses who, with his brother Aaron, confronted Pharaoh time after time and finally conquered Pharaoh and all the power of Egypt. Hebrews 11 reminds us that Moses accomplished all of this by faith in the living God. Passover and the exodus are memorials to the power of faith.

Hebrews 11:27 refers to Exodus 10:28–29 when Pharaoh threatened to kill Moses if he came to see him one more time. Moses believed God's promises and had no fear of what the king might do. Faith simply means that we rely on God and obey His Word, regardless of feelings, circumstances, or consequences.

—*Be Delivered*, page 73

10. Review Hebrews 11:27–29. What are some of the ways that faith inspired and directed Moses along his path to freeing the Jews from Egyptian slavery? What is the direct connection between Jesus' establishment of the Lord's Supper and the Passover that was established during Moses' time? What do both celebrations teach us about the role of faith in everyday living?

## Looking Inward

Take a moment to reflect on all that you've explored thus far in this study of Exodus 11:1—13:16. Review your notes and answers and think about how each of these things matters in your life today.

*Tips for Small Groups: To get the most out of this section, form pairs or trios and have group members take turns answering these questions. Be honest and as open as you can in this discussion, but most of all, be encouraging and supportive of others. Be sensitive to those who are going through particularly difficult times and don't press for people to speak if they're uncomfortable doing so.*

11. What, if anything, troubles you about God's actions toward the reluctant pharaoh? Have you ever heard God's voice and wondered what would happen if you disobeyed? How does Jesus' sacrifice change the way God speaks to His people today?

12. Imagine you were around in the time of the Egyptian captivity. Which would you rather be—a Jew suffering as a slave and awaiting deliverance or an Egyptian enjoying the benefits of power and freedom? What struggles would you have had if you were a Jew and saw time and again how apparently ineffective the plagues were in swaying Pharaoh? What are times in your life today when you feel a similar disappointment or frustration?

13. Moses' faith is probably the most notable aspect of his personal journey throughout this section of Scripture. What appeals to you about Moses' faith? Can you relate to his initial hesitation to do God's will? What are some examples in your own life when you acted on faith? When you didn't act because you didn't have enough faith? What are you doing to actively grow your faith?

## Going Forward

14. Think of one or two things that you have learned that you'd like to work on in the coming week. Remember that this is all about quality, not quantity. It's better to work on one specific area of life and do it well than to work on many and do poorly (or to be so overwhelmed that you simply don't try).

Do you want to work on building a Moses-like faith? Be specific. Go back through Exodus 11:1—13:16 and put a star next to the phrase or verse that is most encouraging to you. Consider memorizing this verse.

*Real-Life Application Ideas: Whether it's the season or not for Passover, arrange to have a Passover meal with your small group or family members. Immerse yourself in the story you've just read, study up on the Passover meal, and then coordinate your own meal. During this time, focus on two things: the historical events that the Passover represents to Jews today, and the symbolism it represents relating to Jesus' sacrifice for us. Enjoy the remembrance and thankfulness together, then try to carry those feelings into the days and weeks to come.*

## Seeking Help

15. Write a prayer below (or simply pray one in silence) inviting God to work on your mind and heart in those areas you've noted in the Going Forward section. Be honest about your desires and fears.

*Notes for Small Groups:*

- *Look for ways to put into practice the things you wrote in the Going Forward section. Talk with other group members about your ideas and commit to being accountable to one another.*

- *During the coming week, ask the Holy Spirit to continue to reveal truth to you from what you've read and studied.*

- *Before you start the next lesson, read Exodus 13:17— 16:36. For more in-depth lesson preparation, read chapters 5, "Redeemed and Rejoicing," and 6, "The School of Life," in* Be Delivered.

# Redeemed
## (EXODUS 13:17—16:36)

*Before you begin …*
- *Pray for the Holy Spirit to reveal truth and wisdom as you go through this lesson.*
- *Read Exodus 13:17—16:36. This lesson references chapters 5 and 6 in* Be Delivered. *It will be helpful for you to have your Bible and a copy of the commentary available as you work through this lesson.*

## Getting Started

### From the Commentary

"It took one night to take Israel out of Egypt, but forty years to take Egypt out of Israel," said George Morrison. If Israel obeyed His will, God would bring them into the Promised Land and give them their inheritance. Forty years later, Moses would remind the new generation, "He [the Lord] brought you out of Egypt ... to bring you in, to give you [the] land as an inheritance" (Deut. 4:37–38 NKJV).

The same thing can be said of the redemption we have in Christ: God brought us out of bondage that He might bring us into blessing. A. W. Tozer used to remind us that "we are saved *to* as well as saved *from*." The person who trusts Jesus Christ is born again into the family of God, but that's just the beginning of an exciting new adventure that should lead to growth and conquest. God liberates us and then leads us through the varied experiences of life, a day at a time, so that we might get to know Him better and claim by faith all that He wants us to have. At the same time, we come to know ourselves better; we discover our strengths and weaknesses, and we grow in understanding God's will and trusting His promises.

—*Be Delivered*, pages 77–78

1. Review Exodus 13:17–22. In what ways was the Israelites' exodus from Egypt not the end of their experience with God, but a new beginning? What are we liberated from today? What is the purpose of that liberation? The result? How are Christians today at a "new beginning" in their experience of God?

*More to Consider: If there had been any military strategists in Israel that night, they probably would have disagreed with the evacuation route God selected because it was too long. Israel's immediate destination was Mount Sinai, so why did two million people take the long way instead of using the shorter and easier route? (The short answer: to avoid other dangers.) Read Proverbs 3:5–6. How does this passage relate to the Jews' path of escape? What are ways God sends us "the long way around" in our faith lives today?*

2. Choose one verse or phrase from Exodus 13:17—16:36 that stands out to you. This could be something you're intrigued by, something that makes you uncomfortable, something that puzzles you, something that resonates with you, or just something you want to examine further. Write that here.

# Going Deeper

## *From the Commentary*

Before he died, Joseph made his brothers promise that, when God delivered Israel from Egypt, their descendants would take his coffin with them to the Promised Land (Gen. 50:24–25; Heb. 11:22). Joseph knew that God would keep His promise and rescue the children of Israel

(Gen. 15:13–16). Joseph also knew that he belonged in the land of Canaan with his people (49:29–33).

Certainly the Jews could look at Joseph's coffin and be encouraged. After all, the Lord cared for Joseph during his trials, and finally delivered him, and He would care for the nation of Israel and eventually set them free. During their years in the wilderness, Israel saw Joseph's coffin as a reminder that God has His times and keeps His promises. Joseph was dead, but he was bearing witness to the faithfulness of God. When they arrived in their land, the Jews kept their promise and buried Joseph with Abraham, Isaac, and Jacob (Josh. 24:32).

—*Be Delivered*, page 79

3. What did Joseph's coffin mean to the generations of Jews who lived during the years of terrible bondage in Egypt? Is it idolatrous to have visible reminders of God's faithfulness? (See Josh. 4; 7:25–26; 24:24–28; 1 Sam. 7:12.) How can such reminders help strengthen our faith?

*From the Commentary*

> The nation was guided by a pillar (column) of cloud by day that became a pillar of fire by night. This pillar was identified with the angel of the Lord who led the nation (Ex. 14:19; 23:20–23; see Neh. 9:12). God occasionally spoke from the pillar of cloud (Num. 12:5–6; Deut. 31:15–16; Ps. 99:7), and the pillar of cloud also shielded the people from the hot sun as they journeyed by day (105:39). When the cloud moved, the camp moved; when the cloud waited, the camp waited (Ex. 40:34–38).
>
> We don't have this same kind of visible guidance today, but we do have the Word of God, which is a light (Ps. 119:105) and a fire (Jer. 23:29). It's interesting to note that the pillar of fire gave light to the Jews but was darkness to the Egyptians (Ex. 14:20). God's people are enlightened by the Word (Eph. 1:15–23), but the unsaved can't understand God's truth (Matt. 11:25; 1 Cor. 2:11–16).
>
> —*Be Delivered*, page 80

4. What's significant about the symbolism of the cloud? Why might God have chosen a cloud to represent Himself? How was this wilderness wandering an act of great faith? What is the "cloud" that leads us today?

## From the Commentary

"He [God] made known His ways to Moses, His acts to the children of Israel" (Ps. 103:7 NKJV). The Jewish people were told what God wanted them to do, but Moses was told why God was doing it. "The secret of the LORD is with them that fear him" (25:14). The leadership of Moses was a key ingredient in Israel's success.

It dawned on Pharaoh and his officers that by allowing their Jewish slaves to escape, they had threatened, if not destroyed, Egypt's whole economy, so the logical thing was to go after the Jews and bring them back. Now we're given another reason why the Lord selected this route: The reports would convince Pharaoh that the Jews were wandering like lost sheep in the wilderness and therefore were fair game for his army to pursue and capture. The Lord was drawing the Egyptians into His trap.

What seemed like an easy victory to Egypt would turn out to be an ignominious defeat, and the Lord would get all the glory. Once again He would triumph over Pharaoh and the gods and goddesses of Egypt. Pharaoh commandeered all the chariots of Egypt, mounted his own royal chariot, and pursued the people of Israel.

—*Be Delivered*, page 81

5. Review Exodus 14:1–31. It seemed like the Egyptians would easily be able to track and recover their escaping slaves. But they didn't count on God's hand. Still, there were moments when it appeared the Israelites were

in trouble. Why was it critical that the Israelites keep their eyes on the fiery pillar? What happened when they took their eyes off the Lord and looked back and saw the Egyptians getting nearer? What's the message in this for us today?

## From the Commentary

With their enemies drowned and their freedom secure, the people of Israel burst into song and praised the Lord. We don't read that they praised God while they were enslaved in Egypt, and while they were going out of the land, they were complaining to Moses and asking him to let them go back. But it takes maturity for God's people to have a "song in the night" (Job 35:10; Ps. 42:8; Matt. 26:30; Acts 16:25), and the Jews were very immature in their faith at that time.

The Lord is mentioned ten times in [the hymn in 15:1–5] as Israel sang to the Lord and about the Lord, for true worship involves faithful witness to who God is and what He has done for His people.

God's victory was a glorious victory, for it was wholly the

work of the Lord. The Egyptian army was thrown into the sea (vv. 1 and 4), and the soldiers sank like stones (v. 5) and like lead (v. 10). They were consumed like burning stubble (v. 7). Pharaoh had ordered the Jewish boy babies to be drowned, so God paid him back in kind and drowned his troops.

The statement "The LORD is a man of war" (v. 3) may upset people who feel that anything relating to warfare is alien to the gospel and the Christian life. Some denominations have taken the "militant" hymns out of their hymnals, including "Onward Christian Soldiers." But Moses promised the people, "The LORD shall fight for you" (14:14; see Deut. 1:30), and one of God's names is "Jehovah-Sabaoth," which means "Lord of hosts, Lord of armies," a title that's used 285 times in the Old Testament.

—*Be Delivered*, page 85

6. Review Exodus 15:1–18. What is the message of each of the four stanzas in this hymn? (See 15:1–5; 6–10; 11–16a; 16b–18.) What does this hymn tell us about God's care for His people? What did it mean to the Israelites that God would fight for His people? What does it mean for us today?

*From the Commentary*

As we trace the activities of the Israelites, we learn some important truths to help us in our own walk of faith.

"Let us be as watchful after the victory as before the battle," wrote saintly Andrew Bonar. It's possible to win the battle and yet lose the victory, which is what the Jews did as they left the Red Sea and began to march toward Mount Sinai. They forgot that life is a pilgrimage during which we must learn new lessons and fight new battles. One great victory doesn't settle everything; we need challenging new experiences that will help us mature and glorify God. Yes, life is a school, and the Lord knows just when to give us an examination.

Uppermost in the minds of the Israelites wasn't how to please God but "What shall we eat?" and "What shall we drink?" According to Jesus, these questions reveal an anxious heart, not a trusting heart (Matt. 6:21, 25–33), and this can lead to all kinds of problems.

A single day in the wilderness without water would be tolerable, two days would be difficult, but three days would be impossible, especially for the children and animals. And then to be disappointed by finding bitter water would only make the situation worse. (The word *Marah* means "bitter" and is related to the word *myrrh*.) But God was testing His people, not because He didn't know their hearts, but because they didn't know their own hearts. People often say, "Well, I know my own heart," but they forget that "the heart is deceitful above all things, and desperately wicked: who can know it?" (Jer. 17:9).

—*Be Delivered*, pages 91–92

7. What is the key difference between the way God tests us and the way Satan tests us? Why did God test the Israelites in the wilderness? What lessons was He teaching? How was this preparation for their lives to come?

*More to Consider: Read Exodus 16:1–12; Numbers 14:2, 27–29; 16:41; 17:1–10; Deuteronomy 1:27; Psalm 78:17–22; 106:14. What do these passages tell us about the Israelites' skill as complainers? How were they tempting God during these times? What would be the right thing to do with concerns like these?*

## From the Commentary

God heard their murmurings and in His grace and mercy met their needs. He told them that in the evening, they would have flesh to eat (v. 8), and in the morning He would rain bread from heaven (v. 4). By giving them these special provisions, He was also testing them to see if they would believe and obey.

In our pilgrim journey through life, we live on promises and not explanations.

As you read the book of Job, you see Job frustrated with God and repeatedly saying, "I'd like to meet God and ask Him a few things!" But when God finally comes to Job, *Job is so overwhelmed he doesn't ask God a thing!* (See Job 40:1–5.) Can we begin to understand the ways and plans of God when His ways are far above us and His wisdom unsearchable (Isa. 55:8–9; Rom. 11:33–36)? Explanations don't heal broken hearts, but promises do, because promises depend on faith, and faith puts us in contact with the grace of God.

—*Be Delivered*, page 95

8. Just like the wandering Israelites, when we hurt, it's a normal response to ask "Why?" Why is that the wrong approach to take? In what ways does asking "why" presume a superior posture to God? Does God have to explain everything to us? Why might He choose not to?

## From the Commentary

> Since God is not the author of confusion (1 Cor. 14:33), whenever He starts something new, He always gives the instructions necessary to make the venture successful. If we obey His instructions, He will bless, but if we disobey, there will be disappointment and discipline. The principle is still "Let all things be done decently and in order" (1 Cor. 14:40).
>
> To begin with, the Jews were instructed to gather their manna daily, but only as much as each person in the family could eat (v. 16). An omer was a Hebrew dry measure equivalent to about two quarts. The manna was especially nutritious because eating it sustained an adult for a day's march in the wilderness. It appears that the members of each family pooled their supply each day and never lacked for sufficient food. Since the Jews marched and camped by tribes (Num. 1—2), no doubt each clan and family pooled the manna they'd gathered and saw to it that everybody was adequately fed.
>
> —*Be Delivered*, pages 97–98

9. In what ways was God's way of providing manna like the ways He provides for us today? In what ways was it different? According to Deuteronomy 8:2–3, what were the Israelites supposed to learn from their experience with manna? Why would daily manna be a good way to learn that? How is this lesson relevant to us?

*From the* **Commentary**

The instructions in 16:33–34 anticipate the giving of the law (or "testimony"; 31:18; 32:15) and the making of the ark of testimony (25:16, 22; 26:33) and the construction of the tabernacle. The information in 16:35 was added years later to complete the account. At that time, Moses wouldn't have known how many years Israel would march in the wilderness.

As we shall see later, the ark of the testimony was the throne of God in the camp. It stood in the Holy of Holies in the tabernacle, where the glory of God dwelt, and within the ark were the two tablets of the law, Aaron's rod, and the golden jar of manna (Heb. 9:4). Only the high priest could enter the Holy of Holies, and that only once a year, but the Jewish people knew what was in the ark and taught this truth to their children. Each of these items reminded the nation of an important truth: that He is King and Lawgiver; that He established the priesthood; and that He fed His people because He cared for them.

God gave the law to Israel because He loved His people. They needed a light to guide them, and God's law is a lamp and a light, and obeying the law means life (Prov. 6:23). When the people disobeyed, they needed a priest to help them be forgiven and reconciled to God. They also needed to be reminded that it was God who provided food for them, and that they didn't live by bread alone but by the Word of God (Deut. 8:1–3).

—*Be Delivered*, pages 99–100

10. Review Exodus 16:32–36. Why would keeping a jar of manna be useful in the years to come? How would it motivate future generations to obey God's commands? What might be the various responses of future generations to that jar of manna?

## Looking Inward

Take a moment to reflect on all that you've explored thus far in this study of Exodus 13:17—16:36. Review your notes and answers and think about how each of these things matters in your life today.

> *Tips for Small Groups: To get the most out of this section, form pairs or trios and have group members take turns answering these questions. Be honest and as open as you can in this discussion, but most of all, be encouraging and supportive of others. Be sensitive to those who are going through particularly difficult times and don't press for people to speak if they're uncomfortable doing so.*

11. Have you ever felt like God was leading you "the long way around" to a hoped-for destination? Why did God lead you that way? What did you learn about yourself along that path? What did you learn about God?

12. When have you complained to God? What circumstances prompted that behavior? What was the result of your complaining? Is there a "right way" to complain to God? What good can come from complaining? What bad?

13. What are some of the "why" questions you've asked God that haven't resulted in answers (yet)? What prompted those questions? Is it arrogant to ask why? Explain. What might be a better question to ask when struggling to understand God's actions (or lack of actions)?

## Going Forward

14. Think of one or two things that you have learned that you'd like to work on in the coming week. Remember that this is all about quality, not quantity. It's better to work on one specific area of life and do it well than

to work on many and do poorly (or to be so overwhelmed that you simply don't try).

Do you want to learn how to better trust God's path, especially when it feels long? Be specific. Go back through Exodus 13:17—16:36 and put a star next to the phrase or verse that is most encouraging to you. Consider memorizing this verse.

*Real-Life Application Ideas: If you don't already journal, begin one today that focuses on "remembering" the ways God has blessed you and directed your path. Don't include just the good things that God has put in your life, but also the challenges He's allowed you to face and learn from. This journal of remembrance can be a great tool for sharing your personal faith story with your children.*

## Seeking Help

15. Write a prayer below (or simply pray one in silence) inviting God to work on your mind and heart in those areas you've noted in the Going Forward section. Be honest about your desires and fears.

*Notes for Small Groups:*

- *Look for ways to put into practice the things you wrote in the Going Forward section. Talk with other group members about your ideas and commit to being accountable to one another.*

- *During the coming week, ask the Holy Spirit to continue to reveal truth to you from what you've read and studied.*

- *Before you start the next lesson, read Exodus 17—18. For more in-depth lesson preparation, read chapter 7, "'The Lord of Hosts Is with Us,'" in* Be Delivered.

# The Lord of Hosts
## (EXODUS 17—18)

*Before you begin …*
- *Pray for the Holy Spirit to reveal truth and wisdom as you go through this lesson.*
- *Read Exodus 17—18. This lesson references chapter 7 in* Be Delivered. *It will be helpful for you to have your Bible and a copy of the commentary available as you work through this lesson.*

## Getting Started

*From the Commentary*

It was the presence of the Lord that gave Moses the strength and confidence he needed as he led the people of Israel during their wilderness wandering. He had a difficult task, leading a thankless army of former slaves whom he was trying to build into a nation, but he persevered because the Lord was with him. The events recorded in these two chapters reveal to us what the presence of the

Lord means to God's people and their leaders as they are on their pilgrim journey.

—*Be Delivered*, page 104

1. Why is the presence of the Lord such an important part of the Israelites' history? What did that presence look like in the garden of Eden? In the days of Abraham? How was that different in Moses' day? How do we experience God's presence today?

2. Choose one verse or phrase from Exodus 17—18 that stands out to you. This could be something you're intrigued by, something that makes you uncomfortable, something that puzzles you, something that resonates with you, or just something you want to examine further. Write that here.

# Going Deeper

*From the Commentary*

As they moved toward Mount Sinai, the people of Israel were still being led by the pillar of cloud by day and the pillar of fire by night. But the Lord was still directing Israel into difficult and trying situations in order to prove His power and build their faith and character. After all, life's journey involves much more than merely reaching a destination. If we aren't growing in faith, in the knowledge of God, and in godly character, we're wasting our opportunities.

Israel had a long way to go before they would qualify as a godly nation. So far, every new trial they experienced only brought out the worst in them. When they arrived in Rephidim, in the wilderness of Sinai, they again found themselves without water. They had failed this test once before, so God had to test them again. He had proved that He was able to provide water and food for them, so why were they quarreling with Moses? *Because their hearts were still in Egypt!* They were guilty of ingratitude and unbelief, wanting to go back to the old life, and as a result, they again failed to pass the test.

—*Be Delivered*, page 104

3. Review Exodus 17:1–3. What are some of the difficulties the wandering Israelites experienced as they moved toward Mount Sinai? How did God use those circumstances to test them? Did that testing make them better

or worse? What determines whether a test from God makes us better or worse?

## From the Commentary

> Moses did what he frequently had to do as a leader: He called on the Lord for help (Ex. 15:25; 32:30ff.; Num. 11:1–2; 12:13; 14:13ff.). "God is our refuge and strength, a very present help in trouble" (Ps. 46:1). The Lord instructed him to take some of the elders with him, plus the rod that symbolized God's power (Ex. 7:20), and to smite the rock in the sight of the people. When Moses obeyed, the water gushed forth from the rock and met the needs of the people and the livestock (Ps. 78:15–16; 105:41; 114:8; Isa. 48:21).
>
> *—Be Delivered*, page 105

4. A "type" is an image or model that prefigures something yet to come. How is the rock that brought forth water a type of Jesus Christ? (See 1 Cor. 10:4.) How is the water a type of the Holy Spirit? (See John 7:37–39.) God provided for the people even though they were complaining. Why did He

do this here and not elsewhere? What message was God giving His people by providing water?

*More to Consider:* Massah *means "to test," and* Meribah *means "contention, quarreling." The Jews had not yet learned that God tests His people in the everyday experiences of life. The Israelite's faith in God was very weak, for they thought their God had led them to a place where He couldn't care for them! Consider how the older generation responded throughout their entire journey from Egypt to Canaan. (See Ps. 95:6–11; Heb. 3; Num. 20:1–13.) What was the error in their thinking? How is this sort of complaining similar to what happens in today's church?*

## From Today's World

Our faith today is tested daily by a myriad of things: by popular media and their often wrong-minded depictions of Christianity; by politics, where sorting through truth and lies forces believers to make difficult decisions about how to act. Then there are the challenges offered by a religious landscape littered with belief systems that all claim to be the truth, some of which appear to be Christian yet incorporate subtle elements that contradict the faith. And finally, there are the everyday challenges of making a living, raising a family, reaching out to friends and strangers. At every corner, our faith may be tested in small or large ways. While most of us probably won't wander in a literal wilderness for forty years, many of us feel as if we're wandering in a figurative one.

5. Why does God still allow so many challenges in our lives today? What are some of the lessons we're learning today that we can't learn simply from studying the challenges of the Israelites, or even the early Christians for that matter? How does God continue to teach us today through challenges? Where are the greatest opportunities for our faith to grow? Why is it important to have a growing faith?

## From the Commentary

On the journey of faith, we not only experience trials involving the necessities of life, such as bread and water, but we also face battles when our enemies attack us. We're pilgrims who are also soldiers, and that means we must occasionally endure hardship as we follow the Lord (2 Tim. 2:3–4).

The Devil is our greatest enemy (1 Peter 5:8), and he uses the world and the flesh to oppose us (Eph. 2:1–3).

Just as Israel was delivered from Egypt by the power of God, so God's people today have been delivered from "this present evil world [age]" (Gal. 1:3–4) through the victory of Christ. We are in the world physically but not of the world spiritually (John 17:14–16), and therefore must not become conformed to the world (Rom. 12:2). We renounce the things of the flesh (Gal. 5:16–21) and resist the attacks of the Devil (James 4:7; 1 Peter 5:8–9).

The Amalekites were the descendants of Jacob's brother, Esau (Gen. 36:12, 16), who was "a profane person" (Heb. 12:16). The word translated "profane" ("godless," NIV) comes from a Greek word that means "a threshold"; it refers to somebody who is accessible and can be "walked on" by anybody or anything. The English word *profane* comes from the Latin and means "outside the temple," that is, unhallowed and common. Esau lived for the world and the flesh and despised spiritual things (v. 17). Esau opposed his brother, Jacob, and threatened to kill him (Gen. 27:41), and Esau's descendants opposed the children of Jacob (Israel) and threatened to annihilate them.

There's no record that the Jews ever had to fight any battles in Egypt, but once they were delivered from bondage, they discovered they had enemies.

—*Be Delivered*, pages 106–107

6. Review Exodus 17:8. What must it have been like for the recently delivered Israelites to discover they had enemies, even as they wandered in

the wilderness? How did their fears affect the way they responded to the uncertainty in their wandering? How were the enemies the Israelites had to battle similar to our call today to "fight the good fight of faith" (1 Tim. 6:12)?

## From the Commentary

Amalek attacked after Israel had experienced a great blessing in the provision of the water from the rock. Satan and his demonic army (Eph. 6:10–12) know what our weakest point is and when we're not ready for an assault. That's why we must "watch and pray, lest [we] enter into temptation. The spirit truly is ready, but the flesh is weak" (Mark 14:38 NKJV).

The enemy often attacks God's people after they've experienced special blessings, but the Lord can use those attacks to keep us from trusting the gifts instead of the Giver. It was after his victory over the four kings that Abraham was tempted to take the spoil (Gen. 14:17–24), and after the victory over Jericho, Joshua became over-confident and was defeated at Ai (Josh. 7). After Elijah defeated the priests of Baal, he became discouraged and was tempted to quit (1 Kings 18:41—19:18), and it was after the blessings at His baptism that our Lord was led into the wilderness to be tempted (Matt. 3:13—4:1). "Therefore let him who thinks he stands take heed lest he fall" (1 Cor. 10:12).

*—Be Delivered*, pages 107–108

7. Read Deuteronomy 25:17–19. What does this passage reveal about the Amalekites' battle plan? How did they attack at the Israelites' "weakest point"? What is our "weakest point" in the church today? How can we guard against attacks?

## From the Commentary

There's no evidence that Israel fought any battles in Egypt. Even on the night of their deliverance from Egypt, they didn't have to fight the attacking Egyptian army because the Lord fought for them. "Stand still, and see the salvation of the LORD which he will show to you today" (Ex. 14:13). But now that they were on their pilgrim journey, Israel would have to enter into battle many times and trust the Lord for victory. "And this is the victory that overcomes the world, even our faith" (1 John 5:4).

This is the first mention of Joshua in the Bible, but he will be named two hundred more times before Scripture ends. He was born in Egypt and named Hoshea, which means "salvation." Later, Moses changed his name to "Joshua—Jehovah is salvation" (Num. 13:8, 16), which is the Hebrew equivalent of "Jesus" (Matt. 1:21; Heb. 4:8). He knew the rigors of Egyptian slavery and must have had an aptitude for military leadership for Moses to make him general of the army. He became Moses' servant (Ex. 24:13; 33:11; Josh. 1:1), for God's policy is that we first prove ourselves as faithful servants before we can be promoted to being leaders (Matt. 25:21, 23). Joshua had only one day to rally his army and get them ready for the attack, but he did it.

—*Be Delivered*, page 108

8. What elements came together to define Israel's great victory over Amalek? What role did God's power play? Joshua's leadership? The intercession of Moses, Aaron, and Hur? God could have sent angels to defeat the Amalekites (Isa. 37:36), but He didn't. Why did he choose to use Joshua and the army instead? How was God glorified in this battle?

*More to Consider: Read Psalms 28:2; 44:20; 63:4; 134:2; 1 Kings 8:22, 38, 54; 1 Timothy 2:8. What do these verses tell us about the significance of Moses holding the staff of God in his hands? Who was actually empowering Joshua and his army: Moses or God? Why did God use Moses in this way?*

## From the Commentary

After reading about the trials, complaints, and battles of the Israelites, it's a relief to move into a chapter that describes the camp of Israel as a quiet place of family fellowship and daily business. Life isn't always hunger and thirst and warfare, although those are often the things we usually remember. Charles Spurgeon said that God's people are prone to engrave their trials in marble and write their blessings in the sand, and perhaps he was right.

But the best thing about this paragraph is that everybody is praising the Lord for all He did for His people. Praising God is much better than complaining to God; in fact, praise is a good antidote for a complaining spirit. "There is a great deal more said in the Bible about praise than prayer," said evangelist D. L. Moody, "yet how few praise-meetings there are!"

—*Be Delivered*, pages 110–111

9. Review Exodus 18:1–12. What does this passage teach us about daily life? Why is it hard for us to remember the good, quiet times and so easy to

remember the difficult times? We often ask where God is during the trials, but where is God during the quiet times? How can we learn to enjoy the quiet, everyday life moments as much as the bigger, louder moments?

## From the Commentary

Moses could have taken a week off and enjoyed his family and entertained his father-in-law, but being a faithful shepherd, he was back the next day helping his people with their problems.

**The task (vv. 13–16).** The nation already had elders (v. 13; 4:29), but they weren't assisting Moses in the day-by-day affairs of the camp, or if they were, there were matters they couldn't settle that had to go to Moses. There were basic regulations for the management of the camp (18:16), since two million people couldn't very well live together and travel together without obeying some kind of code. The phrase *statutes and laws* in verse 16 can refer to the will of God in general as well as to specific ordinances from the Lord. Long before the law was given, God blessed Abraham for obeying His commandments, statutes, and laws (Gen. 26:5).

Judicial codes are necessary for order and security in society, but they always have to be interpreted, even if they come from the Lord. Later, the priests would assist in this task (Mal. 2:4–7), but the priesthood hadn't yet been established. From the time of Ezra (Ezra 7:10), the scribes became the students and interpreters of the law.

**The danger (vv. 17–18).** Jethro knew that Moses' leadership was crucial for the future success of Israel and that any activity that drained his energy or wasted his time was bound to hurt the nation. Also, he didn't want his son-in-law to wear himself out and leave Zipporah a widow and his two grandsons without a father. No one man could minister personally to two million people and last very long. Even after the new arrangement had been established, Moses had to confess that the work was too much for him (Num. 11:14), so what must the burden have been like under the old system? The Hebrew word translated "easier" in Exodus 18:22 means "to take cargo from a ship." ("That will make your load lighter," NIV.)

**The suggestion (vv. 19–27).** Jethro's suggestion was a good one. Moses should organize the camp so that every ten people had somebody to talk to about their civil problems. If a ruler of ten couldn't solve the problem, it could be referred to the ruler of fifty, then one hundred, and then one thousand. After that, it would be referred to Moses himself. D. L. Moody may have had this in mind when he said, "I would rather put ten men to work than do the work of ten men."

—Be Delivered, pages 112–113

10. Why was Moses' leadership crucial to the future success of Israel? How is the way Jethro suggested they organize the camp similar to the way churches are organized today? What were the primary benefits of sharing the load? Why is that important for leaders today? What happens to a leader when he or she fails to delegate responsibilities?

## Looking Inward

Take a moment to reflect on all that you've explored thus far in this study of Exodus 17—18. Review your notes and answers and think about how each of these things matters in your life today.

> *Tips for Small Groups: To get the most out of this section, form pairs or trios and have group members take turns answering these questions. Be honest and as open as you can in this discussion, but most of all, be encouraging and supportive of others. Be sensitive to those who are going through particularly difficult times and don't press for people to speak if they're uncomfortable doing so.*

11. The presence of the Lord gave Moses strength during difficult times. What are ways you experience the presence of God in your life today?

What does God's presence look like to you? If you don't experience that presence, what are some practical steps you can take to change that?

12. When has your faith been attacked at your weakest point? What are your weak points? How can you gird those areas of your faith life so attacks there are more easily turned away?

13. What are some of the ways you worship God during the mundane parts of life? How do you stay connected to God during those times?

## Going Forward

14. Think of one or two things that you have learned that you'd like to work on in the coming week. Remember that this is all about quality, not quantity. It's better to work on one specific area of life and do it well than to work on many and do poorly (or to be so overwhelmed that you simply don't try).

Do you want to invite God's presence more often? Be specific. Go back through Exodus 17—18 and put a star next to the phrase or verse that is most encouraging to you. Consider memorizing this verse.

*Real-Life Application Ideas: Invite a discussion in your church about the structure and systems. Don't do this with intent to tear things apart just for the sake of change, but only to determine if there are things you (and others) can do to be even more efficient in ministry. This might include evaluation of small-group size and coordination, evangelism strategies, and other ministry activities. Keep in mind that the goal to is to unburden leaders who are doing too much, not burden them with more responsibilities.*

## Seeking Help

15. Write a prayer below (or simply pray one in silence) inviting God to work on your mind and heart in those areas you've noted in the Going Forward section. Be honest about your desires and fears.

*Notes for Small Groups:*
- *Look for ways to put into practice the things you wrote in the Going Forward section. Talk with other group members about your ideas and commit to being accountable to one another.*
- *During the coming week, ask the Holy Spirit to continue to reveal truth to you from what you've read and studied.*
- *Before you start the next lesson, read Exodus 19:1— 24:8. For more in-depth lesson preparation, read chapters 8, "Hear the Voice of God," and 9, "The Book of the Covenant," in* Be Delivered.

# The Book
## (EXODUS 19:1—24:8)

*Before you begin ...*
- *Pray for the Holy Spirit to reveal truth and wisdom as you go through this lesson.*
- *Read Exodus 19:1—24:8. This lesson references chapters 8 and 9 in* Be Delivered. *It will be helpful for you to have your Bible and a copy of the commentary available as you work through this lesson.*

## Getting Started

*From the Commentary*

If freedom doesn't lead to maturity, then we end up imprisoned in a bondage worse than what we had before, a bondage from within and not from without. It's bad enough to be enslaved by an Egyptian taskmaster, but it's even worse to enslave yourself and become your own taskmaster.

Moses went up to meet God on the mountain, and what God told him, he came down and shared with the people.

The image of maturity that God used was that of the eagle, bearing its young on its wings and teaching them the glorious freedom of flight. Moses used the same image in the song he taught Israel at the close of his life.

From God's point of view, Egypt was a furnace of affliction for Israel (Deut. 4:20; 1 Kings 8:51; Jer. 11:4), but the Jews often saw Egypt as a "nest" where they at least had food, shelter, and security (Ex. 16:1–3; Num. 11:1–9). God delivered them from Egypt because He had something better for them to enjoy and to do, but this meant that they had to "try their wings" and experience growing pains as they moved toward maturity.

—*Be Delivered*, page 120

1. Read carefully Deuteronomy 32:10–12. What do eagles teach us about the life of maturity? What does true freedom really mean? How does true freedom deliver us from doing bad things? How does true freedom help us accomplish God's will?

2. Choose one verse or phrase from Exodus 19:1—24:8 that stands out to you. This could be something you're intrigued by, something that makes

you uncomfortable, something that puzzles you, something that resonates with you, or just something you want to examine further. Write that here.

## Going Deeper

*From the Commentary*

> In Egypt, the Jews were nothing but weary bodies, slaves who did their masters' bidding, but the Lord had better things planned for them. They were to be His special people, and He would use them to be a blessing to the whole world (Gen. 12:3).
>
> All the nations of the earth belong to the Lord, because He's their Maker and their Sustainer (Ex. 9:29; Ps. 24:1; 50:12; Acts 14:15–17; 17:24–28), but He's chosen Israel to be His treasured possession (Deut. 7:6; 14:2; 26:18; Ps. 135:4; Mal. 3:17).
>
> —*Be Delivered*, page 121

3. Why did God choose Israel as His special people? (See Deut. 7:6–8; 9:4–6; 26:5–11.) In what ways were they supposed to be a blessing to the

nations (Gen. 12:3; 22:18)? How does this apply today, after Jesus' sacrifice? What does it mean for Christians today?

*More to Consider: "Be holy, for I am holy" is found at least six times in Leviticus (11:44–45; 19:2; 20:7, 26; 21:8) and is repeated twice in 1 Peter 1:15–16. How does this phrase speak to the idea of Israel's special status before God? What implications did holiness have for their lifestyle? What implications does holiness have for us today? What does it look like in practical terms?*

## From the Commentary

Moses had returned to the Lord on the mountain and reported the people's promise to obey His commandments. The fact that God spoke with Moses personally should have given the people confidence in their leader, but subsequent events proved differently. What a privilege it was for Israel to have a leader such as Moses, and what a tragedy that they repeatedly made life difficult for him!

The emphasis in this chapter is on the sanctity of the nation as the holy people of God, and three images stand out: the changing of their clothes, the distance set between the people and God, and the storm on Mount Sinai.

—*Be Delivered*, pages 123–124

4. How does each of the images noted above illustrate the sanctity of God's people? (See 19:9–25.) Why is the sanctity of God's people important to God? To the world? Why is being "set apart" such a huge theme in this part of Scripture?

## From the Commentary

The privilege of freedom brings with it the responsibility to use that freedom wisely for the glory of God and the good of others. However, the Ten Commandments were much more than laws for governing the life of the nation of Israel. They are part of the covenant God made with Israel when He took them to Himself to be His special people (Ex. 6:1–8; 19:5–8). In the Abrahamic covenant,

God gave the Jews the title deed to the Promised Land (Gen. 12:3; 13:14–18), but Israel's possession and enjoyment of that land depended on their obedience to the Mosaic covenant. The tragedy is that the nation disobeyed the law, defiled their land, and grieved their Lord, so they had to be chastened.

The law was never given as a way of salvation for either Jews or Gentiles, because "by the works of the law shall no flesh be justified" (Gal. 2:16). Salvation is not a reward for good works but the gift of God through faith in Jesus Christ (Rom. 4:5; Eph. 2:8–9). The law reveals God's righteousness and demands righteousness, but it can't give righteousness (Gal. 2:21); only Jesus Christ can do that (2 Cor. 5:21). The law is a mirror that reveals where you're dirty, but you don't wash your face in the mirror (James 1:22–25). Only the blood of Jesus Christ can cleanse us from sin (1 John 1:7, 9; Heb. 10:22).

—*Be Delivered*, pages 125–126

5. Review Exodus 20:1–17. Why did God choose to give the Israelites the Ten Commandments? In what ways was obedience to these commandments a response to God's grace? Why might some of the Jews have come to believe that "salvation" was a product of following the rules? If not because of the law, why does God give His Spirit to us (Gal. 3:2; 4:1–7)?

## From the Commentary

An idol is a substitute for God and therefore not a god, for there is only one true and living God. Present-day religious pluralism ("You worship your god and I'll worship mine, because both are right") is both unbiblical and illogical, for how can there be more than one god? If God is God, He is infinite, eternal, and sovereign and can't share the throne with another being who is also infinite, eternal, and sovereign.

"I am the LORD: that is my name; and my glory I will not give to another, neither my praise to graven [carved] images" (Isa. 42:8). The idol worship of the pagan nations was not only illogical and unbiblical, but it was intensely immoral (temple prostitutes and fertility rites), inhuman (sacrificing children), and demonic (1 Cor. 10:10–22). No wonder the Lord commanded Israel to destroy the temples, altars, and idols of the pagans when they invaded the land of Canaan (Deut. 7:1–11).

"Little children, keep yourselves from idols" (1 John 5:21) was the apostle John's final admonition to Christians in his day, and the admonition needs to be heeded today. If an idol is anything that takes the place of God, anything to which we devote our energy and time, or for which we make sacrifices because we love it and serve it, then John's warning is needed today. The idols that entice God's people today are things like money, recognition, success, material possessions (cars, houses, boats, collectibles), knowledge, or even other people.

God is so serious about receiving exclusive worship and love that He punishes those who refuse to obey Him.

—*Be Delivered*, pages 127–128

6. What does it mean that God is a "jealous God"? Read Ezekiel 23. Why does Ezekiel compare idolatry to prostitution? What do they have in common? Read Jeremiah 2:13. How is idolatry like digging your own water cistern? Why do people go after false gods like money and recognition if those things are like cisterns with holes?

## From the Commentary

The word *sabbath* means "rest." The Sabbath tradition was already a part of Israel's life (Ex. 16:23, 25), but now it became a part of Israel's law and their covenant relationship with God. While the Sabbath was rooted in creation (Gen. 2:1–3), it was also a special sign between Israel and the Lord (Ex. 31:12–17; Neh. 9:13–15; Ezek. 20:12, 20), and there's no biblical evidence that God commanded any Gentile nation to observe the seventh day (Ps. 147:19–20). Later, Moses associated the Sabbath with Israel's deliverance from Egypt (Deut. 5:12–15), a foretaste of the rest they would enjoy in their promised inheritance (3:20; 12:10; 25:19).

—*Be Delivered*, page 129

7. What did it mean for the Jews to observe the Sabbath? What did doing so say about their relationship with God? In what ways was it a witness to others? What does the Sabbath reveal about the importance of taking care of ourselves and others who work hard, as well as honoring God?

*From the Commentary*

Forty years later when Moses reviewed the law with the new generation, he reminded them that their ancestors had seen manifestations of God's glory and power at Sinai and heard His words, but they *"saw no form of any kind"* (Deut. 4:15 NIV). God didn't reveal Himself in any form lest the Jews turn the living God into a dead idol. "To whom then will you liken God? Or what likeness will you compare to Him?" (Isa. 40:18 NKJV).

The Jews were called to be a people of the Word. The success of the nation depended on hearing God's Word, believing it, and obeying it. The nations around Israel built their religions on what they could see—idols made by men's hands, but Israel was to worship an invisible God and have nothing to do with idols.

The Jewish scholar Abraham Joshua Heschel summarized Israel's theology of the Scriptures when he wrote, "To believe, we need God, a soul, and the Word."

God warned Israel not to manufacture idols and not to build elaborate altars such as those used by the heathen nations around them (see 2 Kings 16:10–20). A simple altar of earth or unhewn stone would be acceptable to the Lord. If the stones were chiseled, they would become like idols, and the work of man would become more important than the worship of God. The natural stone provided by the Lord was all He would accept.

—*Be Delivered*, pages 135–136

8. Respond to this quote from Christian philosopher Jacques Ellul: "False gods are always gods one can see (and touch), and that very quality demonstrates their falsity and their nonexistence as gods." What are the touchable and visible gods that we encounter today? How do they compete for our attention with the one true God?

*More to Consider: Both nudity and intercourse with temple prostitutes were a part of many pagan religious ceremonies, and these were expressly forbidden by the Lord. How did God deal with this particular issue? Read Exodus 28:42–43; Leviticus 6:10. And consider the punishment if they didn't obey: Exodus 28:35, 43.*

*Still, Israel quickly disobeyed these commandments while Moses was on the mountain. Why did they so quickly turn to pagan rituals? What did they think they would gain by this? What was the actual result? (See Ex. 32:1–6, 25–29.)*

### From the Commentary

> Justice is the practical outworking of the righteousness of God in human history, for the Lord loves "righteousness and justice" (Ps. 33:5; see Isa. 30:18; 61:8). There may be a great deal of injustice in our world today, but the time will come when God will judge the world in righteousness by the Savior whom the world has rejected, and His judgment will be just (Acts 17:31).
>
> —*Be Delivered*, page 137

9. Review the various laws outlined in Exodus 21:1—23:19. Choose three or four of them and talk about the purpose each of these laws served. What concerns did each law address? How do these laws reflect timeless principles of justice?

## From the Commentary

The Israelites would remain at Sinai about eleven months, and then they would journey to Kadesh-Barnea, where they were to enter the land (Num. 10:11—14:45). Failing to trust God and claim their inheritance, they were condemned to journey in the wilderness until the generation twenty years old and upward had all died, except for Caleb and Joshua. For thirty-eight years, God would guide His people and then bring them back to the borders of Canaan to enter and claim the land.

The angel here is Jesus Christ, the Son of God, the Angel of the Covenant (Ex. 14:19). Only He can pardon transgressions and only in Him is the wonderful name of the Lord. God had prepared a place for His earthly people (23:20) just as Jesus is preparing a place for His heavenly people (John 14:1–6). If they followed the Lord, He would meet all their needs and defeat all their enemies.

Once again, the Lord warned them about the sin of idolatry, worshipping the false gods of the nations around them, the nations that they would defeat. If Israel devoted themselves wholly to the Lord, He would go before them, confound their enemies, and enable them to conquer the land. Indeed, the "terror of God" did go before Israel and weaken the people in the land (Josh. 2:11; Ex. 15:16). The "hornet" in 23:28 could well have been the insect that we know, because the people of the East respect the hornet (Deut. 7:20; Josh. 24:12). The Hebrew word is similar to the word for Egypt (*zirah/mizraim*), so some students believe that the reference is to the Egyptian armies that frequently invaded Canaan before the Jews arrived. In Isaiah 7:18, Egypt is compared to a fly and Assyria to a bee.

—*Be Delivered*, page 146

10. Why did God punish the Israelites by making them wander for forty years? What does this teach us about God's nature? Why did it take Joshua and his armies seven years to occupy the land? What was the point of taking the land gradually, instead of all at once?

## Looking Inward

Take a moment to reflect on all that you've explored thus far in this study of Exodus 19:1—24:8. Review your notes and answers and think about how each of these things matters in your life today.

*Tips for Small Groups: To get the most out of this section, form pairs or trios and have group members take turns answering these questions. Be honest and as open as you can in this discussion, but most of all, be encouraging and supportive of others. Be sensitive to those who are going through particularly difficult times and don't press for people to speak if they're uncomfortable doing so.*

11. What does it mean for you to be holy? How do you pursue holiness? What is the line that separates true holiness from a holier-than-thou attitude? How do you avoid the latter while working on the former?

12. What are some ways you are set apart because of your faith in Christ? How does that play out in practical ways? How do you find balance to be both set apart and also very much a part of the world in which you live? Why are both important to a life of faith?

13. What is one of the idols you struggle with? How does it steal from your relationship with God? What are some practical ways to overcome the temptations of this idol?

# Going Forward

14. Think of one or two things that you have learned that you'd like to work on in the coming week. Remember that this is all about quality, not quantity. It's better to work on one specific area of life and do it well than to work on many and do poorly (or to be so overwhelmed that you simply don't try).

Do you want to pursue holiness in some area of your life? Be specific. Go back through Exodus 19:1—24:8 and put a star next to the phrase or verse that is most encouraging to you. Consider memorizing this verse.

*Real-Life Application Ideas: A big part of this section of Exodus focuses on laws and on the breaking of those laws. This week, take some time to consider all the laws you encounter (or enforce) in your life. This could be everything from a stop sign to the rules of the house (everyone eats dinner together; beds must be made; etc.) to the rules and regulations relating to your work. As you look at each rule, think about the reason it was enacted. If you discover some rules that seem counterproductive, consider relaxing them or discussing with the appropriate people what it might look like to change them. Rules have a purpose (as the Jews*

*discovered in both good and bad ways), but if they get in the way of*
*growing your faith, they might just be bad rules.*

## Seeking Help

15. Write a prayer below (or simply pray one in silence) inviting God to work on your mind and heart in those areas you've noted in the Going Forward section. Be honest about your desires and fears.

*Notes for Small Groups:*

- *Look for ways to put into practice the things you wrote in the Going Forward section. Talk with other group members about your ideas and commit to being accountable to one another.*

- *During the coming week, ask the Holy Spirit to continue to reveal truth to you from what you've read and studied.*

- *Before you start the next lesson, read Exodus 24:9— 27:21; 30—31; 35—38. For more in-depth lesson preparation, read chapters 10, "The Place Where God Dwells—Part I," and 11, "The Place Where God Dwells—Part II," in* Be Delivered.

# Where God Dwells

## (EXODUS 24:9—27:21; 30—31; 35—38)

*Before you begin ...*

- *Pray for the Holy Spirit to reveal truth and wisdom as you go through this lesson.*
- *Read Exodus 24:9—27:21; 30—31; 35—38. This lesson references chapters 10 and 11 in* Be Delivered. *It will be helpful for you to have your Bible and a copy of the commentary available as you work through this lesson.*

## Getting Started

### From the Commentary

Faithful to His promises in Exodus 6:6–8, the Lord delivered His people from Egypt (Ex. 1—18) and at Sinai "adopted" them to Himself as His special treasure (Ex. 19—24; Rom. 9:4). Now He was about to fulfill the rest of that promise by coming to the camp of Israel to dwell with His people (Ex. 25—40).

In order to do this, the Lord needed two things: a place for His glory to dwell and servants to minister to Him in that place. Therefore, He commanded the Jews to build the tabernacle and to set apart the tribe of Levi to serve Him. The building of the tabernacle and the ordaining of the priesthood are the two major themes of Exodus 25—40.

Throughout the book of Genesis, the Lord had walked with His people—Adam and Eve (3:8), Enoch (5:22–24), Noah (6:9), and the patriarchs (17:1; 24:40; 48:15), but now He would *dwell* with them (Ex. 25:8, 45–46; 29:44–46). Having the Lord dwelling in the camp was a great privilege for the nation of Israel (Rom. 9:4–5), for no other nation had the living God in their midst. But the privilege brought with it a great responsibility, for it meant that the camp of Israel had to be a holy place where the holy God could dwell.

—*Be Delivered*, page 153

1. What do these chapters teach us about the construction of the tabernacle? Why would God include all this historical construction detail in Scripture? What spiritual truths are revealed in this section?

2. Choose one verse or phrase from Exodus 24:9—27:21; 30—31; 35—38 that stands out to you. This could be something you're intrigued by, something that makes you uncomfortable, something that puzzles you, something that resonates with you, or just something you want to examine further. Write that here.

# Going Deeper

*From the Commentary*

> Worshipping God is the highest privilege and the greatest responsibility of the Christian life, because God is the highest Being in the universe and the One to whom we must one day give account. Everything that we are and do flows out of our relationship with the Lord. God created us in His image so we might love Him and have fellowship with Him, not because we have to but because we want to. God is seeking people who will worship Him "in spirit and in truth" (John 4:23–24).
>
> At the base of the mountain, taking care not to get too close, the people of Israel waited for the words of the Lord. Moses, Aaron, Nadab and Abihu, and the seventy elders ascended higher and met with the Lord (Ex. 24:9–11),

and then Moses and Joshua moved even higher (vv. 13–14). Finally, Moses alone went up higher and there saw the glory of the Lord (vv. 15–17).

*—Be Delivered*, page 155

3. Review Exodus 24:9–18. How is this an illustration of the importance of growing in our worship experience of God? Why do so many people settle for the lowest expression of worship? What are the most dramatic differences between our worship experience today and the worship experience described here? (See Heb. 10:19–25.)

*More to Consider: When Scripture says that the seventy-four men "saw … God," this doesn't mean they beheld God in His essential being, for this isn't possible (John 1:18). They saw some of God's glory, and they probably saw the throne of God on the sapphire pavement (see Ezek. 1:26), but the invisible God was hidden from them. Why is it important that God remained hidden from them? Why did He choose not to reveal Himself? What did the men do after the encounter? How is this a model we can apply to encounters with God today?*

## From the Commentary

> Whenever God does a work, He has a plan for that work, whether it's building the tabernacle or the temple (1 Chron. 28:11–12, 18–19), a local church (Phil. 2:12–13), or the individual Christian life and ministry (Eph. 2:10). God warned Moses to make everything according to the pattern revealed to him on the mount (Ex. 25:40; Heb. 8:5).
>
> —*Be Delivered*, page 156

4. Review Exodus 25:9, 40; 26:30. In what ways is the earthly tabernacle a copy of the heavenly tabernacle? (See Heb. 8:1–5; 9:1; Rev. 6:9–11; 8:3–5; 4:2, 4–7.) Why is it notable that these two tabernacles are so similar? What are other ways God connects our earthly experience of Him with the heavenly truth?

*From the Commentary*

> We can give to God only that which He has first given
> to us, for all things come from Him. "Everything comes
> from you," said David in his prayer, "and we have given
> you only what comes from your hand" (1 Chron. 29:14
> NIV).
>
> Not only did God create the materials that the people
> brought to Him (Isa. 66:1–2), but He also worked in their
> hearts so that they were willing to give generously (see 2
> Cor. 8:1–5, 12). In fact, the people brought so much that
> Moses had to tell them to stop (Ex. 36:6–7)!
>
> Several different kinds of materials were needed: precious
> metals (gold, silver, and bronze), fabrics (yarn, fine linen,
> and goat's hair), wood, skins, olive oil, spices, and pre-
> cious stones. It's been estimated that a ton of gold was
> used in the tabernacle as well as over three tons of silver.
> Where did all this wealth come from? For one thing, the
> Jews had "spoiled" the Egyptians before leaving the land
> (12:35–36), and no doubt there were also spoils from the
> victory over Amalek (17:8–16). God saw to it that they
> had everything they needed to build the tabernacle just as
> He had designed it.
>
> —*Be Delivered*, page 157

5. What does God's provision for the tabernacle teach us about God?
About His plans for His people? How does this picture of God's provision
relate to God's provision for His church today?

## From the Commentary

There were six special pieces of furniture associated with the tabernacle and the ark of the covenant is mentioned first. A wooden chest forty-five inches long, twenty-seven inches wide, and twenty-seven inches high, it stood in the Holy of Holies, where God's "shekinah" presence rested. On it rested the golden mercy seat, which was God's throne (Ps. 80:1; 99:1; 2 Kings 19:15, all NIV).

The ark had many names besides "the ark of the covenant" (Num. 10:33). It was called "the ark of God" (1 Sam. 3:3), "the ark of the Lord" (Josh. 3:15), "the ark of the LORD God" (1 Kings 2:26), "the ark of the testimony" (Ex. 25:22), because the tables of the law were in it, "the holy ark" (2 Chron. 35:3), and "the ark of [God's] strength" (Ps. 132:8).

—*Be Delivered*, page 158

6. What did the ark represent? What meanings do the different names point to? How does it point toward what Christ did (Heb. 9:3–12)?

## From the Commentary

The altar of incense was made of acacia wood overlaid with gold, and was a foot and a half square and three feet high. It was the tallest piece of furniture in the Holy Place. It had an ornamental gold rim ("crown") around the top and golden "horns" at each corner. It stood before the veil that separated the Holy of Holies from the Holy Place, and the priest burned incense on it each morning and evening when he trimmed the lamps.

In the Bible, burning incense is often a picture of prayer. "Let my prayer be set forth before thee as incense," David prayed (Ps. 141:2), and John saw the elders in heaven with "golden bowls full of incense, which are the prayers of the saints" (Rev. 5:8 NIV; see 8:3–4). Whenever the priest burned the incense, it was a call to the people for a time of prayer (Luke 1:8–10).

*—Be Delivered*, pages 167–168

7. Why did the fire for burning the incense come from the altar where the sacrifices were offered to God (Lev. 16:12–13; Num. 16:46)? What does this suggest about the source and purpose of our prayer? In what ways is prayer a blessing that God sends down to us? What does effective prayer look like? (See James 5:13–18.)

*More to Consider: The priests were warned not to use this golden altar for anything other than burning incense (Ex. 30:9), for there are no substitutes for prayer. The golden altar wasn't a place for making bargains with God or trying to change His mind (James 4:1–4; 1 John 5:14–15). It was a place for adoring Him and praying, "Thy will be done."*

*It's worth noting that the special incense had to be "salted" (Ex. 30:35). What was the purpose for this? (See Lev. 2:13.) Why are we commanded to lift up "holy hands" as we pray (1 Tim. 2:8)?*

## From the Commentary

When a worshipper came to the tabernacle to offer a sacrifice, the first thing he met was a white linen fence, 150 feet long and seventy-five feet wide, that surrounded the tabernacle and created a courtyard area where the priests ministered. The tabernacle proper stood at the west end of this courtyard, and at the east end was a thirty-foot entrance to the enclosure. Here the priests met the people who came to offer sacrifices and examined each animal carefully to make sure it was acceptable. The worshipper would put his hand on the animal's head to identify with the offering (Lev. 1:1–9), and then the priest would slay the animal and offer it on the brazen altar, according to the regulations given in Leviticus 1—7.

—*Be Delivered*, pages 169–170

8. Why was there only one entrance to the tabernacle? What was the symbolism of this? How does our access to God today compare to the tabernacle? (See John 10:9; 14:6; Prov. 14:12; 16:25; Matt. 7:13–27.)

## From the Commentary

> Preachers and evangelists sometimes invite people in their congregations to "come to the altar," but there are no altars on earth that are ordained of God or acceptable to God. Why? Because the death of Jesus Christ took care of the sin problem once and for all (Heb. 9:25–28). No more sacrifices can be or should be offered. The Lord's Supper (Communion, Eucharist) is a reminder of His sacrifice, not a repeat of His sacrifice.
>
> The only "altar" believers have today is Jesus Christ Himself, who bears on His glorified body the wounds of the cross (Heb. 13:10; Luke 24:39; John 20:20). As a holy priesthood, believers "offer up spiritual sacrifices acceptable to God *through Jesus Christ*" (1 Peter 2:5 NKJV). We present to Him our bodies (Rom. 12:1–2), our material wealth (Phil. 4:18), praise and good works (Heb. 13:15–16), and a broken heart (Ps. 51:17).
>
> —*Be Delivered*, page 171

9. What would it have been like to give an animal to a priest and watch the animal sacrificed on the altar for your sake? What effect was that supposed to have on a worshipper? How should the sacrifice of Jesus have a similar and/or different effect on us? How can our worship include equally vivid reminders of what Jesus has done?

## From the Commentary

"Honor and majesty are before him," wrote the psalmist; "strength and beauty are in his sanctuary" (Ps. 96:6). The strength of His sanctuary is revealed in its *construction*, and the beauty is revealed in its *adornment*.

**Strength.** The tabernacle proper was a solid structure over which the beautiful curtains were draped. Twenty boards of acacia wood, fifteen feet high and twenty-seven inches wide, overlaid with gold, formed the north and south walls, and eight similar boards formed the west wall. Each of these boards stood on two silver bases made from the shekels ("redemption money") collected from the Jewish men of military age. Since the structure stood on the uneven ground, these bases were necessary for stability and security. God's sanctuary didn't rest on the shifting sands of this world but on the solid foundation of redemption. The forty-eight boards were further strengthened by four long rods (crossbars) that ran through golden rings on each board.

**Beauty.** Gold, blue, purple, scarlet, and white are the major colors used in the hangings and coverings of the tabernacle. The linen fence around the sacred area was white, reminding us of the holiness of God. The thirty-foot gate at the east end of the tabernacle was embroidered with blue, purple, and scarlet against the white background. Blue is the color of the sky and reminds us of heaven and the God of heaven. Purple is the royal color that speaks of the King, and scarlet makes us think of blood and the sacrifice of the Savior.

**Appreciation.** No matter how common the tabernacle may have appeared to outsiders, everything within the sanctuary was costly and beautiful, and it all spoke of the Savior, whom the people of Israel would give to the world.

—*Be Delivered*, pages 173–174

10. Review Exodus 26:1–37; 27:9–19; 36:8–38; 38:9–20. Why did God commission a tabernacle that was so beautiful? What message did that beauty present to the people? What did it reveal about God?

# Looking Inward

Take a moment to reflect on all that you've explored thus far in this study of Exodus 24:9—27:21; 30—31; 35—38. Review your notes and answers and think about how each of these things matters in your life today.

*Tips for Small Groups: To get the most out of this section, form pairs or trios and have group members take turns answering these questions. Be honest and as open as you can in this discussion, but most of all, be encouraging and supportive of others. Be sensitive to those who are going through particularly difficult times and don't press for people to speak if they're uncomfortable doing so.*

11. How has your worship changed since you first met Christ? Are there ways you worship today that you never would have back then? What have you learned about what it means to worship God as you've grown in your faith?

12. Describe your prayer life. What are the nonnegotiables in your prayer life? What are some ways you can grow your prayer life?

132 \ The Wiersbe Bible Study Series: Exodus

13. The altar was an important part of the connection the Jews had to God. What are some of the symbols that you find helpful in your own faith experience? How do they help you grow closer to God?

## Going Forward

14. Think of one or two things that you have learned that you'd like to work on in the coming week. Remember that this is all about quality, not quantity. It's better to work on one specific area of life and do it well than to work on many and do poorly (or to be so overwhelmed that you simply don't try).

Do you want to deepen your worship? Be specific. Go back through Exodus 24:9—27:21; 30—31; 35—38 and put a star next to the phrase or verse that is most encouraging to you. Consider memorizing this verse.

*Real-Life Application Ideas: The tabernacle was a very real place where certain people met God. But today, it is a symbol of that connection to God. Is there a place or places where you go regularly to spend time in God's presence? How is that place like a tabernacle to you? Or is place not important to you in your worship? This week, go somewhere to meet with God, and approach Him there as if you are entering His holy presence—because you are.*

## Seeking Help

15. Write a prayer below (or simply pray one in silence) inviting God to work on your mind and heart in those areas you've noted in the Going Forward section. Be honest about your desires and fears.

*Notes for Small Groups:*

- *Look for ways to put into practice the things you wrote in the Going Forward section. Talk with other group members about your ideas and commit to being accountable to one another.*

- *During the coming week, ask the Holy Spirit to continue to reveal truth to you from what you've read and studied.*

- *Before you start the next lesson, read Exodus 28—29; 32—34; 39—40. For more in-depth lesson preparation, read chapters 12, "The Holy Priesthood," and 13, "A Broken Heart and a Shining Face," in* Be Delivered.

# Glory
## (EXODUS 28—29; 32—34; 39—40)

*Before you begin …*

- *Pray for the Holy Spirit to reveal truth and wisdom as you go through this lesson.*
- *Read Exodus 28—29; 32—34; 39—40. This lesson references chapters 12 and 13 in* Be Delivered. *It will be helpful for you to have your Bible and a copy of the commentary available as you work through this lesson.*

## Getting Started

*From the Commentary*

It was God's desire that the nation of Israel be "a kingdom of priests" (Ex. 19:6) in the world, revealing His glory and sharing His blessings with the unbelieving nations around them. But in order to magnify the holy God, Israel had to be a holy people, and that's where the Aaronic priesthood came in. It was the task of the priests (Aaron's family) and the Levites (the families of Kohath, Gershon, and Merari; see Num. 3—4) to serve in the tabernacle and represent the people before God. The priests were also to represent God to the people by teaching them the law and helping them to obey it (Lev. 10:8–11; Deut. 33:10; Mal. 2:7).

But Israel failed to live like a kingdom of priests. Instead, the spiritual leadership in the nation gradually deteriorated until the priests actually permitted the people to worship idols in the temple of God (Ezek. 8)! The Lord punished His people by allowing the Babylonians to destroy Jerusalem and the temple and carry thousands of Jews into exile. Why did this happen? "But it happened because of the sins of her prophets and the iniquities of her priests, who shed within her the blood of the righteous" (Lam. 4:13 NIV).

Today, God wants His church to minister in this world as a "holy priesthood" and a "royal priesthood" (1 Peter 2:5, 9).

—*Be Delivered*, page 179

1. How is God's plan for today's church similar to His plan for the Israelites? In what ways does God want His church to minister like a holy and royal priesthood? (See 1 Peter 2:5, 9.) What does that look like in practical terms?

*More to Consider: That God chose Aaron and his sons to minister in the priesthood was an act of sovereign grace, because they certainly didn't earn this position or deserve it. What does this reveal to us about God? How is this same grace at the core of our relationship with Christ today? (See John 15:16 NKJV.)*

2. Choose one verse or phrase from Exodus 28—29; 32—34; 39—40 that stands out to you. This could be something you're intrigued by, something that makes you uncomfortable, something that puzzles you, something that resonates with you, or just something you want to examine further. Write that here.

# Going Deeper

*From the Commentary*

In serving God and the people, the high priest wore seven pieces of clothing: undergarments (vv. 42–43); a white inner robe ("coat," v. 39; 39:27; Lev. 8:6–7); a blue robe over that, with bells and pomegranates on the hem (Ex. 28:31–35; 39:22–26); the ephod, a sleeveless garment of gold, blue, purple, and scarlet, held together by a jeweled clasp on each shoulder (28:6–8; 39:1–5; Lev. 8:7); a girdle at the waist (Ex. 28:8); a jeweled breastplate held in place on the ephod by golden chains attached to the shoulder clasps (vv. 9–30; 39:8–21); and a white linen turban ("miter," 28:39) with a golden plate on it that said "HOLY TO THE LORD" (v. 36 NIV).

"Ephod" is the transliteration of a Hebrew word for a simple sleeveless linen garment that reached to the ankles, usually associated with religious service (1 Sam. 2:18; 2 Sam. 6:14). The high priest's ephod and girdle were made of white linen beautifully embroidered with blue, purple, and scarlet threads. The ephod was of two pieces, front and back, held together on each shoulder by a jeweled golden clasp and at the waist by the beautiful girdle.

The significant thing about this ephod was not the fabric or the colors. It was that the names of six tribes of Israel were engraved on each onyx stone on the shoulder clasps, according to their birth order. Whenever the high priest wore his special robes, he carried the people on his shoulders before the Lord. Furthermore, these two onyx stones reminded him of two important facts: (1) The tribes of Israel were precious in the sight of God; (2) he wasn't in the tabernacle to display his beautiful robes or to exalt his special position, but to represent the people before the Lord and carry them on his shoulders. He had been called, not to serve himself but to serve his people.

If the church is to be faithful as a holy priesthood, believers must serve Christ by serving one another and serving a lost world. Jesus said, "I am among you as the One who serves" (Luke 22:27 NKJV), and it's His example that we should follow (John 13:12–17). In the high-powered spiritual atmosphere of the tabernacle, it would be easy for the priest to ignore the common people outside, many of whom had burdens and problems and needed God's help. "Let each of you look out not only for his own interests, but also for the interests of others" (Phil. 2:4 NKJV).

—*Be Delivered*, pages 181–182

3. Review Exodus 28:6–30; 39:2–21. How is today's holy priesthood different from the priesthood that was created during the events of Exodus? What is the role of the church as holy priesthood today?

## From the Commentary

Moses enumerates some additional articles of clothing.

The blue robe (28:31–35; 39:22–26), worn under the ephod, was distinctive in at least three ways. For one thing, it was seamless, reminding us of our Lord's seamless robe, which symbolized His perfect character and integrity (John 19:23). The collar around the opening for the head was woven so that it would not tear. During our Lord's ministry on earth, some people tried to "tear" the seamless robe of His character and accuse Him of wrong, but they never succeeded. Finally, around the hem of this garment hung pomegranates made of blue, purple, and scarlet yarn, with golden bells hanging between them. The pomegranates symbolized fruitfulness and the golden bells gave witness that the high priest was ministering in the Holy Place. The bells and pomegranates remind us that our priestly walk must be fruitful and faithful, always giving witness that we're serving the Lord with integrity.

The turban (28:36–38; 39:27–31) was worn only by the high priest, while the other priests wore linen bonnets. At the front of the turban was the golden plate that read "Holiness to the Lord" ("Holy to the Lord," NIV).

—*Be Delivered*, page 184

4. What was the primary purpose of the Levitical system? How did people become holy under this system? How is that different because of Jesus' life, death, and resurrection? Respond to this statement: Jesus didn't die to make us happy; He died to make sinners holy.

## From the Commentary

God commanded that the high priest and his sons participate in a public consecration service that would set them apart as God's servants. There were at least seven stages in this service.

**The priests were washed (Ex. 29:4; Lev. 8:6).** Moses gathered the materials that were needed for the ordination service and brought Aaron and his sons to the door of the tabernacle. The erecting of the tabernacle isn't described until Exodus 40, but it appears that the dedication of the tabernacle and the consecration of the priests occurred on the same day (vv. 12–15).

**The priests were clothed (Ex. 29:5–6, 8–9, 29–30; Lev. 8:7–9, 13).** Moses clothed his brother with the garments we've been studying, and he also clothed Aaron's sons with their linen tunics and bonnets. These were their official "uniforms," and they dared not minister in the tabernacle dressed in other garments.

In Scripture, the wearing of garments is a picture of the character and life of the believer. We're to lay aside the filthy garments of the old life and wear the beautiful "garments of grace" provided by the Lord (Eph. 4:17–32; Col. 3:1–15).

**The priests were anointed (Ex. 29:7, 21; Lev. 8:10–12, 30).** This special oil (Ex. 30:22–33) was used only to anoint the priests and the tabernacle and its furnishings. In the Old Testament, prophets, priests, and kings were anointed; it was a symbol that God had granted them the Holy Spirit for power and service (Luke 4:17–19; Isa. 61:1–3). Moses poured the oil on his brother's head, which meant it ran down his beard and therefore bathed all the stones on the breastplate. What a beautiful picture of unity in the Lord (Ps. 133:2)! "Would God that all the LORD's people were prophets, and that the LORD would put his spirit upon them!" (Num. 11:29).

**The priests were forgiven (Ex. 29:10–14).** A bull was slain as a sin offering (Lev. 4; 8:14–17) to atone for the sins of the priests. This sacrifice was repeated each day for a week (Ex. 29:36–37) not only for the cleansing of the priests but also for the sanctifying of the altar where the priests would be ministering. Jesus Christ is our sin offering and through Him alone we find forgiveness (Isa. 53:4–6, 12; Matt. 26:28; 2 Cor. 5:21; 1 Peter 2:24; Rev. 1:5–6).

**The priests were completely dedicated to God (Ex. 29:15–18; Lev. 8:18–21).** In the sacrifice of the burnt offering, the animal was completely given to the Lord, a picture of total dedication (Lev. 1). Our Lord gave Himself fully and without reservation, not only in His ministry before the cross, but in His willing sacrifice of Himself on the cross. The high priest and his associates were expected to devote themselves wholly to the work of the ministry and to make it the uppermost concern of their hearts.

**The priests were marked by the blood (Ex. 29:19–22; Lev. 8:22– 24).** At this point in the ordination ceremony, we would have expected Moses to offer a trespass offering (Lev. 5), but instead, he offered a ram as a peace offering, "the ram of consecration" (Ex. 29:22 NIV, "ordination"). The Hebrew word means "filling" because the priests' hands were filled with the bread and meat.

**The priests were fed (Ex. 29:22–28, 31–34; Lev. 8:25–29).** Another unique occurrence was the filling of the priests' hands from the "food basket" (Ex. 29:2–3) and from the altar (vv. 22–28). The priests waved these gifts toward the altar in dedication to God (v. 24, the "wave offering") and then shared them in a fellowship meal (vv. 31–34).

*—Be Delivered*, pages 186–189

5. What did it mean for the priests to be consecrated? Why were they set apart in a way different from the common man or woman? How are these priests similar to and different from our church leaders today?

*From the Commentary*

> During the week of ordination ceremonies, the priests had
> to remain in the tabernacle precincts, and when the week
> ended, they immediately entered into their ministry. No
> time for a day off or a vacation! In their work, they had to
> follow a daily, weekly, monthly, and yearly schedule, all
> of which was outlined in the law that God gave Moses on
> Mount Sinai.
>
> Each day would begin with the priests sacrificing a lamb
> as a burnt offering, signifying the total dedication of
> the people to God, and the day ended with the offering
> of a second lamb as a burnt offering. With each lamb,
> they also presented a meal offering mixed with oil (Lev.
> 2:1–16; 6:14–23) and a drink offering of about a quart of
> wine, which was poured on the altar (Num. 15:1–13). For
> most meal offerings, the priests put only a token portion
> of the flour on the altar and used the rest in their own
> meals, but with the daily morning and evening sacrifices,
> this wasn't done. Everything was given to the Lord.
>
> The flour and wine represented the results of the people's
> labor in the fields and the vineyards. Symbolically, they were
> presenting the fruit of their toil to God and thanking Him
> for the strength to work and for food to eat (Deut. 8:6–18).
> The wine poured out was a picture of their lives poured out
> in His service (Phil. 2:17; 2 Tim. 4:6, both NIV). All of this
> would please the Lord and He would find delight in dwell-
> ing in the tabernacle and blessing His people.
>
> —*Be Delivered*, pages 189–190

6. Routine was carefully prescribed for the priests. What was the purpose of such detailed and strict guidelines? The priests opened and closed each day with surrender to God. How could we benefit from a similar approach to our faith lives today? What are some of the things the priests did then that we all do now?

## From the Commentary

At least three times during the months at Sinai, the Jewish people had promised to obey whatever God told them to do (Ex. 19:8; 24:3, 7; and see 20:19). The Lord knew that it wasn't in their hearts to keep their promises (Deut. 5:28–29), and the tragedy of the golden calf proved Him right.

Moses called what they did "a great sin" (Ex. 32:21, 30–31), and his assessment was accurate. It was a great sin because of who committed it: the nation of Israel, the chosen people of God, His special treasure. It was great because of when and where they committed it: at Mount Sinai after they had heard God's law declared and seen God's glory revealed. They had promised to obey God's law, but in making a golden calf and indulging in a sensual celebration, the nation broke the first, second, and seventh commandments. It was a great sin because of what they had already experienced of the power and mercy of God: the judgments against Egypt, the deliverance at the Red Sea, the provision of food and water, and the gracious leading of God by the pillar of cloud and fire. What they did was rebel against the goodness of the Lord. It's no wonder their sin provoked God to anger (Deut. 9:7).

—*Be Delivered*, page 194

7. Why did the Israelites commit such an evil act at such a glorious time in their history? What role did impatience play in their decision? To what degree were Aaron and the tribal leaders to blame for what happened? What does this teach us about the responsibility of all leaders?

## From the Commentary

During the second period of forty days and nights with God on Mount Sinai, Moses pled for the people and asked the Lord to restore His promised blessings to them.

Moses reminded the Lord of His promise to accompany the people on their journey. In fact, when the nation sang God's praises at the Red Sea, they rejoiced in the promise of God's victorious presence (Ex. 15:13–18). Was God now going to go back on His word?

Moses based his appeal on the grace (favor) of God, for he knew that the Lord was merciful and gracious and that the people were guilty. If God gave them what they deserved, they would have been destroyed! The Jews were God's people and Moses was God's servant. They didn't want an angel to accompany them, for there was nothing special about that. The thing that distinguished Israel from the other nations was that their God was present with them, and that's what Moses requested. His heart must have leaped for joy when he heard God promise to accompany the people and lead them to the place of rest that He had promised.

*—Be Delivered*, pages 198–199

8. Do God's children have the right to negotiate with God as Moses did? Explain. Why did Moses have that right? (See Ps. 103:7.) What is our role today as advocates of God's people?

*More to Consider: Faith comes by hearing and receiving God's Word (Rom. 10:17), so Moses by faith asked God to forgive the people. Why did Moses use the inclusive "our" in his prayer (Ex. 34:9)? How is this similar to the confessional prayers of Ezra and Daniel? (See Ezra 9; Dan. 9.)*

## From the Commentary

The book of Exodus opens with Moses seeing God's glory in the burning bush (3:1–5), and it closes with the glory of God descending into the camp and filling the tabernacle. The presence of the glory of God in the camp of Israel was not a luxury; it was a necessity. It identified Israel as the people of God and set them apart from the other nations, for the tabernacle was consecrated by the glory of God (29:43–44). Other nations had sacred buildings, but they were empty. The tabernacle of Israel was blessed with the presence of the glory of God.

Moses had been fasting and praying in the presence of God for eighty days, and he had seen a glimpse of God's glory. Is it any wonder that he had a shining face? He didn't realize that he had "absorbed" some of the glory and was reflecting it from his countenance. Because of this glory, the people were afraid to come near him, but he summoned them to come and they talked as before. However, after he was finished speaking to the people, Moses put on a veil to cover the glory.

—*Be Delivered*, page 201

9. Review Exodus 34:29–35; 39:32—40:38. Why did Moses wear a veil? (See 2 Cor. 3:13.) Why was it important that the people not see the fading glory of God? Read 2 Corinthians 3. What applications does Paul make of this remarkable event?

*From the Commentary*

> When you read Jewish history, you discover that the glory that once dwelt in the tabernacle departed from it when the priests and the people sinned against the Lord (1 Sam. 4:21–22). *Ichabod* means "the glory is gone." When Solomon dedicated the temple, God's glory once again came to dwell with His people (1 Kings 8:10–11), but once again their sins drove God's glory away (Ezek. 8:4; 9:3; 10:4, 18; 11:23).
>
> The next time the glory of God came to earth was in the person of Jesus Christ (John 1:14). In the Greek translation of the Old Testament (the Septuagint), the word *abode* in Exodus 40:35 is the Greek word used in Luke 1:35 and translated "overshadow." Mary's virgin womb was a Holy of Holies where the glory of God dwelt in the

person of God's Son. What did the world do with this glory? Nailed it to a cross!

—*Be Delivered*, pages 203–204

10. God's glory used to dwell in the tabernacle. Where is God's glory today? (See 1 Cor. 3:10–23; 6:19–20; Eph. 2:20–22.) What is heaven's promise of God's glory? (See Rev. 21:23.) Where does God live today? (See Acts 7:48–50.)

## Looking Inward

Take a moment to reflect on all that you've explored thus far in this study of Exodus 28—29; 32—24; 39—40. Review your notes and answers and think about how each of these things matters in your life today.

> *Tips for Small Groups: To get the most out of this section, form pairs or trios and have group members take turns answering these questions. Be honest and as open as you can in this discussion, but most of all, be encouraging and supportive of others. Be sensitive to those who are going through particularly difficult times and don't press for people to speak if they're uncomfortable doing so.*

11. Do you consider yourself a "priest" according to the description of the modern church as a "holy priesthood"? Why or why not? What does Jesus' sacrifice mean to you, in terms of your journey to holiness? How do you pursue holiness today?

12. The Jewish people were impatient with Moses. Describe a time when you were impatient with God. What prompted that impatience? What was the result of your impatience? Why is it important to always wait on God, even when it seems God isn't saying anything at all?

13. What are some ways you experience God's glory today? How do you glorify God? Why is that important to your relationship with God?

## Going Forward

14. Think of one or two things that you have learned that you'd like to work on in the coming week. Remember that this is all about quality, not quantity. It's better to work on one specific area of life and do it well than to work on many and do poorly (or to be so overwhelmed that you simply don't try).

Do you want to work on becoming more patient with God? Be specific. Go back through Exodus 28—29; 32—34; 39—40 and put a star next to the phrase or verse that is most encouraging to you. Consider memorizing this verse.

*Real-Life Application Ideas: God's glory is not confined to a building today. It's found in His people. This week, simply pay attention to that truth—that God is glorified through people just like you! Allow that truth to be present with you in all interactions with family members, friends, and coworkers. Knowing God is not only presemt with you always, but also glorified through you, can have a positive, life-changing effect on your day.*

## Seeking Help

15. Write a prayer below (or simply pray one in silence) inviting God to work on your mind and heart in those areas you've noted in the Going Forward section. Be honest about your desires and fears.

*Notes for Small Groups:*

- *Look for ways to put into practice the things you wrote in the Going Forward section. Talk with other group members about your ideas and commit to being accountable to one another.*

- *During the coming week, ask the Holy Spirit to continue to reveal truth to you from what you've read and studied.*

# Summary and Review

*Notes for Small Groups: This session is a summary and review of this book. Because of that, it is shorter than the previous lessons. If you are using this in a small-group setting, consider combining this lesson with a time of fellowship or a shared meal.*

*Before you begin…*
- *Pray for the Holy Spirit to reveal truth and wisdom as you go through this lesson.*
- *Briefly review the notes you made in the previous sessions. You will refer back to previous sections throughout this bonus lesson.*

## Looking Back

1. Over the past eight lessons, you've examined the book of Exodus. What expectations did you bring to this study? In what ways were those expectations met?

2. What is the most significant personal discovery you've made from this study?

3. What surprised you most about Exodus? What, if anything, troubled you?

## Progress Report

4. Take a few moments to review the Going Forward sections of the previous lessons. How would you rate your progress for each of the things you chose to work on? What adjustments, if any, do you need to make to continue on the path toward spiritual maturity?

5. In what ways have you grown closer to Christ during this study? Take a moment to celebrate those things. Then think of areas where you feel you still need to grow and note those here. Make plans to revisit this study in a few weeks to review your growing faith.

## Things to Pray About

6. Exodus is a book about deliverance. As you reflect on this theme, consider how you have been delivered, not by Moses, but by Jesus' death and resurrection.

7. The messages in Exodus include faithfulness, redemption, trust, God's presence, and God's glory. Spend time praying about each of these topics.

158 \ The Wiersbe Bible Study Series: Exodus

8. Whether you've been studying this in a small group or on your own, there are many other Christians working through the very same issues you discovered when examining Exodus. Take time to pray for each of them, that God would reveal truth, that the Holy Spirit would guide you, and that each person might grow in spiritual maturity according to God's will.

## A Blessing of Encouragement

Studying the Bible is one of the best ways to learn how to be more like Christ. Thanks for taking this step. In closing, let this blessing precede you and follow you into the next week while you continue to marinate in God's Word:

*May God light your path to greater understanding as you review the truths found in Exodus and consider how they can help you grow closer to Christ.*

# GETTING FREE
## IS ONLY HALF THE STORY

Part of Dr. Warren W. Wiersbe's bestselling "BE" commentary series, *BE Delivered* has now been updated with study questions and a new introduction by Ken Baugh. A respected pastor and Bible teacher, Dr. Wiersbe explores the need to balance freedom with responsibility. Filled with real-world examples that resonate today, this study uncovers how you can experience true freedom in every area of your life.

David C Cook
transforming lives together